MW00416040

More Praise for
Breath of God

I have spent recent hours observing *Breath of God*. I scrolled through its entirety, dropping down every now and again to read closely a paragraph, a story, or a quote and always experienced a rush of life and excitement. "Why this rush?" I ask myself. My only offered answer is that everywhere I stopped to read. I saw life in a deeper dimension and God in a clearer perspective. *Breath of God* is comprised of dozens of relevant quotes from household names—even Yogi Berra—along with brilliant "one-liners" from Eddie's pen, establishing a body of truth through Scripture that exposes many of the evil and destructive ideas that are hovering over our polluted society. Eddie, in a few strategically chosen words, lays them deservedly to rest. Dear reader, be prepared to laugh, cry, feel deeply, be convicted, and see further than ever before as you read this remarkable book.

Jack Taylor
President, Dimensions Ministries
Melbourne, Florida

———◦•◦◦•◦———

Breath of God is a call back to the Garden of Eden and the Father's original plan for *you*. It is a call back to the purpose for which you were created (your spiritual DNA). This book has genuine revelation and insight. It is a journey in understanding your Heavenly Father's heart and His loving plan for your life. Sit back, relax, and begin to read...the Holy Spirit is about to answer many questions about your destiny.

Jay Comiskey
Vice President of Support Operations
Christian Broadcasting Network

———◦•◦◦•◦———

Breath of God is a beautiful picture of God's original bond with man and how He desires to restore that intimacy to its purest form.

Lenny LeBlanc
Worship Leader
Dove-Winning Christian Recording Artist

———◦•◦◦•◦———

How exciting it is to know what you have been created for and the destiny of God upon your life! God is breathing fresh revelation at this hour to those who have an ear for what the Spirit is saying to the church. Dr. Eddie Lawrence has had an ear to hear, and he takes us back to the beginning where God first breathed upon mankind and set the course of destiny to live in the presence of the Lord. You must know your destiny in order to move forward. Let God breathe afresh upon your life as you hear the voice of God through this book.

Tammy L. Alsup
Kingdom Alignment International

Ever doubted God's love for you? You won't ever again after you read this book about His breath on you. A fascinating and revealing reading! Life-changing!

Quin Sherrer
Author
Miracles Happen When You Pray

BREATH OF GOD

UNLEASHING THE FATHER'S PRESENCE INTO YOUR LIFE

DR. EDDIE LAWRENCE

NELSON BOOKS
A Division of Thomas Nelson Publishers
Since 1798

www.thomasnelson.com

Published in Nashville, Tennessee, by Thomas Nelson, Inc.
www.thomasnelson.com

Nelson Books titles may be purchased in bulk for educational, business,
fundraising, or sales promotional use. For information, please email
SpecialMarkets@ThomasNelson.com.

Unless otherwise stated, all Scripture passages are from The New King
James Version (NKJV®), copyright 1979, 1980, 1982, Thomas Nelson, Inc.,
Publishers.

Text design/composition by Rainbow Graphics, Kingsport, Tennessee

Breath of God

ISBN: 0-5291-2274-X

Printed in the United States of America

1 2 3 4 5 6 — 09 08 07 06

CONTENTS

CONTENTS

SECTION FOUR
Father's Home in You

SECTION FIVE
Father's Home for You

To fall in love with God is the greatest of all romances;
To seek Him, the greatest adventure;
To find Him, the greatest human achievement.

Raphael Simon

APPRECIATION

As every author comes to understand, it takes a lot of effort to finish a project. There is certainly a thrill in rounding third base and finally sliding into home plate. However, every run scored is truly a team effort. I am so grateful to my wife, Mikki, and my children, Andrew, Kara Beth, Elliott, and Nathan, for sacrificing so that I could write. They are each an incredible inspiration to me in ways that a thousand books this size could not describe.

A big "Thank You!" goes to Dr. R. T. Kendall for his encouraging words about this book and his encouraging words spoken into my life. Whenever I have asked him questions, he has always been very honest, yet very affirming. I respect you, Dr. Kendall.

I also want to express my gratitude to Sandra Harper and Marie Lewey for their help in reading and offering suggestions to improve this work.

A very special *"Thank You!"* goes to Carlene Blackburn, an instructor of English as a Second Language from the University of North Alabama, for her help in proofing and editing this work for me.

Thanks to Wes Harbour with Nelson Ministry Services for his encouragement and assistance to me and for his belief in and passion for the *Breath of God* message. Also, I would like to thank Ramona Richards for helping me make this a better book.

Of course, I must express my gratitude to the wonderful congregation, leadership, and staff which I have the privilege of pastoring. You have supported and encouraged and allowed me to invest the time necessary to complete this assignment. Thank you! It is such a blessing to walk in your midst.

*Art is a collaboration between God and the artist,
and the less the artist does the better.*

André Gide

DEDICATION

I want to dedicate this book to my dad and my mom. Dad has gone to be with our heavenly Father. I am so grateful to be able to say that I never had a moment when I doubted my father's love for me. What an incredible blessing he was to me! Likewise, my mom has always nurtured me, loved me, and believed in me. Thank you, Mom! I have always cherished knowing you love me. I am grateful you have experienced the breath of God and the Lord has blessed you with Bob, a wonderful husband to you, and a loving stepdad for my sister, Deb, and me. Deb, thanks for being my "Sis." We had exciting moments growing up together. Your love has never waned toward me. Thanks to you and Tony for always cheering for your kid brother.

FOREWORD

Once in a blue moon a book comes along from a person generally unknown to the world, but who should be heard because of their fresh, original thinking. Dr. Eddie Lawrence's *Breath of God* is such a book. It deserves to be read by all Christians—also by non-Christians—because this book is ideal as an evangelistic tool as well.

When I read a book, I often ask, "Would I want my children to read this? Is this a book a non-Christian could read and understand? Is it theologically sound? Is it honoring to God? Does it edify one's spirit?" When putting these questions to *Breath of God*, the answer is "Yes." It is sound, easy reading but creative and imaginative.

What gripped me was that Dr. Lawrence has asked questions I had not even thought of! He looks carefully at the account of creation in the Book of Genesis and puts questions to the text that are new to me. He then gives answers that are both sensible and edifying. This is a serious, no-nonsense book that reflects a heart after God. He makes you appreciate God as Father, as well as the Holy Spirit through whom we have fellowship with God, and the importance of the family as being in the mind of God from the beginning. This book will make you want to worship and praise God. You may want to read it on your knees. Dr. Lawrence is to be congratulated for providing us with this book.

R. T. Kendall
Minister, Westminster Chapel (1977-2002)
London

Call to Me, and I will answer you,
and show you great and mighty things, which you do not know.
Jeremiah 33:3

INTRODUCTION

To some people, life is no more than a long ride that starts fast and slows to a grinding halt. Like a fly riding on a ceiling fan that's afraid to jump off, they just ride life and wait for it all to stop. Is that all life is—two periods with a line in between? Life is a journey. But a journey that is doing more than just making big circles around the boulevard of time until the clock stops ticking. Life has been ordained to carry you somewhere. That "somewhere" is the place that philosophers, theologians, and whittlers in front of old country stores like to talk about. I invite you on a journey. I will share with you where the journey begins and where it continues because it really never ends. The only requirement on your part is to strap in and ride with me. We are going to talk about you, your destiny, and how much God has always been involved in your life. We will spend time in the Garden of Eden where our ancestors had their start. We will spend time studying about the womb in which you were developed. You will be reintroduced to the familiar and surprised by what you may not have considered previously. You will be taught about Adam's first word, what Eve did before she met Adam, the part of you that existed before you became the *you* who you now are, and many more exciting nuggets. From Adam's first breath to Jesus' last breath, you will see an intriguing pursuit of God after your heart. You will be told what you have in common with a steeple on a church roof. You will learn what the four rivers that flowed out of Eden have in common with your life. We will even discuss how many times God thinks about you every time the clock ticks. The heart of this book is really about your heart, God's heart, and how to bring the two together.

One Friday afternoon, while everyone at my children's school celebrated Grandparents Day, I witnessed an event that ignited a spark of insight within me. I asked my wife for pen and paper so I could jot down some of the thoughts that flooded my mind. These thoughts started me on a journey that has culminated in this book.

You would need to be a pharmacist or have the gift of interpretation to read the notes I scribbled that day. I hope that these "notes" are a little clearer now.

God is the giver of the breath of life. The breath that you have been given came from God. Every time you breathe, you are experiencing a gift from God. Each day of your life, you will experience an average of 25,920 respirations. That is a lot of breathing. However, there is only one first breath experience in your natural life. Adam, the first man who ever lived, experienced the *first* first breath. The moment when Adam breathed for the first time forms the basis of this book. Just as a person's first breath starts them on an exciting journey in the world that surrounds them, the breath of God can come at other times in other ways to launch you on a new adventure. There can be recurring occasions when the Spirit of God moves upon you and suddenly your plans are changed and your life is changed.

In the Bible, the terms *wind, spirit,* and *breath* are used interchangeably. We see the wind of God moving in power all through the Scriptures. God literally breathed Adam into existence. The wind began to blow when Moses held his rod over the sea, and it prepared a way for God's people to move toward the land of their destiny. In the treetops above him, David heard the wind of the Spirit producing the sound of marching soldiers. This was given to him as a sign of his impending victory. In the book of Ezekiel, the Prophet saw the wind of the Spirit blow upon dry bones and they began to stand up and live. Jesus told a religious leader asking sincere but serious questions about God, that the ministry of the Holy Spirit was like the blowing of the wind. Prior to Jesus' ascension, He breathed on His disciples and told them to receive the Holy Spirit. On the day of Pentecost, the sound of a rushing mighty wind filled the place where the disciples were praying and the church was birthed. It changed everything! This is the power of the breath of God. The breath of God begets first things and new beginnings. This same breath is still sweeping across people's lives changing them in dramatic ways. The loving breath of God can be breathed upon you as well.

While growing up, I attended a small high school in a rural area of Alabama. I learned a lot at Brilliant High School. Yes, that's right, Brilliant was the name. Therefore, I jokingly tell my wife that she has a *brilliant* husband. Above the door of our principal's office was a sign that read, "It's what you learn after you know it all that counts." I really didn't understand what that sign meant until I was invited to the principal's office one day. I will not embarrass myself further by telling you why I was there. Let's just say that he and I had a little meeting at which he applied the board of education to the seat of learning and it resulted in the acquisition of knowledge in my life. As I gingerly walked out under the sign, I realized that I wasn't as *brilliant* as I had thought, and I understood a little more of what that sign meant. There are times in all of our lives when we have wake-up calls, confrontations, and encounters that challenge what we think we have always known. This is certainly true when it comes to the truth of who God is and how He works in our lives.

It is important that we are open to all the truth contained in the Scriptures concerning what God desires to do in our lives. As St. Augustine wrote, "If you believe what you like in the gospels, and reject what you don't like, it is not the gospel you believe, but yourself." I regret the times I have chosen what I would believe or not believe based on personal preference instead of biblical revelation. At one time, I had a closed mind about what the Holy Spirit wanted to do in my life. How vain for me to have thought I could control the wind! I have since chosen to tear up several of the boxes that I had tried to use to contain God. God boxes don't work too long or too well. Actually, our God boxes are just walls we build around our own lives that do not allow the breath of God to be breathed on us. I have learned a lot after I thought I knew it all. I have learned that God will not be bound by the interpretation of any group. People can argue until they are blue in the face about who God is and how He works in our lives, but while they argue, God will just go on being Himself. Knowing God personally is the best way to learn about who He is. There is a sea of difference between the words "conceptually" and "personally." I do not worship a concept; I worship a living supreme being who is God. People can form their own conceptions about who I am, but it doesn't change who I am. God, when answering Moses' question about who He was, simply said, "I AM." He still is, by the way! I encourage all of us to keep pressing toward Him to know Him for who He is. Let's not limit ourselves to knowing Him second-hand.

I hope that your journey through the pages of this book will result in a new discovery about something with which you are most likely very familiar—the creation of the first man, Adam. Sometimes certain Bible verses can become so familiar that we lose the grandeur of the truth they contain. At other times, our familiarity with them causes us to assume that we already know what they are saying. The story of Adam's first breath is filled with fascinating insights that give us understanding about our lives. Adam truly was a brilliant man, but he lived and breathed and got into trouble just like we do. His life was designed to experience God-given destiny. So was yours!

It is my prayer that the message of truth contained in this book will help you to know how much God desires to enjoy you, and how much you can enjoy Him. Whether you are a Christian or not, this book will help you understand some things about God and yourself that will encourage and help you. Your destiny is something that you were given to enjoy. It is God's gift to you. That is what *Breath of God* is all about. In this book, you will be given fresh insights to help you understand who God created you to *be* and what He created you to *do*.

There may be times we laugh together and cry together, but we will have a good time. I believe you will experience God in a way that differs from what you have experienced before. I believe you will enjoy the stories and anecdotes that illustrate powerful Scriptural truths. I challenge you to allow your view of God to become more personal and intimate. After you are buckled up, I encourage you to take a deep breath, relax, and *hang on!* Ready yourself for the *Breath of God* experience.

SECTION ONE

FATHER'S HAND ON YOU

ONE

A LIFE LESS GOD

≈❧≈

*If I find in myself desires which nothing in
this world can satisfy,
the only logical explanation is that I was
made for another world.*

C.S. Lewis

If you are going to believe in God, be passionate about it! I want to
be a spur in the flank of the advancing kingdom of God. Most
atheists are more passionate about their *rejection* of God than believers are about their *acceptance* of God. A lifeless version of anything
is hardly admired by anyone. It is what we are willing to die for that
defines us. If what you are living for is not worth dying for, then
there is a place in your heart where you have drawn a line in the
sand and are standing against your own destiny. "God" can be a
generic term, but God never intended to have a generic relationship
with you. He wants the real thing. I believe that you do too, or you
would not be holding a book such as this in your hands! I pray that
if there is gunpowder in you to be lit, that this book will provide the
spark. There is another world to live for, but we must use this one
to find it. Samuel Rutherford, who drew his breath in this world
during the seventeenth century, testified, "Alas, we but chase feath-
ers flying in the air, and tire our own spirits, for the froth and over-
gilded clay of a dying life. One sight of what my Lord hath let me
see within this short time is worth a world of worlds." There is an

experience and encounter with God that is beyond description of man's language. It defies the analysis of man's reason and can only be discovered through the periscope of faith that dares to penetrate the realm of the unseen. You may soak in your spa, sweat in your sauna, or lounge by your pool, but nothing can remove that gnawing pain deep in your gut that says, "There is a God, and one day I will have to face Him." The truth is that He wants you to face Him now and know Him now. When you do, the gnawing pain becomes genuine peace.

God can be known so much more intimately than most of us have thought. Our passionate pursuit of Him will lead us to the place of intimacy with Him. We tend to possess what we pursue. If you truly want to know God, pursue Him. We cannot be fulfilled in our lives with anything less than God. We must realize anything less than God misses the mark of our true destiny and identity. God made us for Himself. The unfortunate result of a life lived *less God* is a *godless* life. The next sad state of being is to serve a lifeless god. A life less God or a lifeless god are both tragic in their consequences. The true God is a God of life. He is a life-giving God. Where He is there is life! The title deed to humanity belongs to God. Augustine put it like this: "Our souls are restless, O God, 'til they find their rest in Thee." Each of us has our point of origin within God Himself, and we should make it our aim to see Him as our final destination. From everlasting to everlasting, He is God! Whether we are looking back at our history or forward to our destiny, we should realize that we find the meaning of our past and the purpose of our future in God Himself. You did not spontaneously generate and appear in your mother's arms one day. There were processes that preceded your arrival and those processes were put into place by___God_____. How would you finish the previous sentence? Your answer actually places a sentence upon your life. Do you sentence yourself to a life less God? Or, do you sentence yourself to a life with God? If you did not put God in the blank, I hope this book will encourage you to do so. There are a lot of blanks in people's lives that if filled with "God" would add so much meaning to their existence. You did not arrive here solo. Someone has had you on His mind for a long time. He made Adam, and He made you. He made you both for the same purpose.

The journey of life is best lived when it is lived in partnership with God. Our lives are smaller when we leave God out. D. L.

Moody said, "If God is your partner, make your plans *BIG!*" This is good advice. This partnership is much more intimate than you might think. It is not like a contractual business partnership where two parties operate independently and both share in the mutual profits. It is a partnership of the Greater with the lesser where the Greater is the Father and the lesser is you, the child. The love of the Greater for the lesser is the driving force of the relationship. This enables the lesser one to experience the greatness of the Greater One. This entering into the greatness of the Greater One is called "destiny." We find our destiny in God Himself.

Blaise Pascal (1623-1662), a French philosopher known primarily for his research in physics and chemistry, also wrote about God. An often-repeated statement, which originated with him, is, "Within each one of us there is a God-shaped vacuum that only God can fill." This is true. We were made in the image of God and until that image is properly reflected within us, we are living below the level of our Heavenly Father's intention. A person who settles for a life without God settles for a lesser existence. Contentment with anything less than God Himself is like cotton candy. It may appear to have substance to it, but it is very short lived; it is quickly gone. He is the Creator; we are the created. He developed the plan; we are the result of that plan. He had a purpose that motivated His plan; that purpose tells us why we are here. This plan and purpose greatly pleases God. Not only were we made *by* Him, but we were also made *for* Him.

Thou art worthy, O Lord, to receive glory and honour and power: for thou hast created all things, and for thy pleasure they are and were created (Re 4:11, KJV).

Wow! You and I were created for God's pleasure. God has been pleased to extend to us the invitation to experience true purpose and pleasure in our lives. We live because of Him. We move because of Him. We have being because of Him. We are His offspring. We are just gropers until we find Him; then, we discover He was there all the time, but we did not see Him or know Him. How sad for people to flounder all the days of their lives. How sad to spend days vainly looking for the meaning of life while just one step of faith away from true destiny. The Apostle Paul once addressed a group of philosophers who spent their days speculating and debating about the meaning of life. Here is part of what he told them:

. . . so that they should seek the Lord, in the hope that they might grope for Him and find Him, though He is not far from each one of us; for in Him we live and move and have our being, as also some of your own poets have said, 'For we are also His offspring.'

Acts 17:27-28

At this very moment, He is not far from you. God never intended that you were to live aloof from Him. He has never been too far from you. He intends that you live, move, and be in Him. You were created to belong to Him, and He wants you to know it. He desires a close relationship with you, and as He reveals His heart to you, you will be fascinated and ruined for anything else. He is life's grand purpose for you. He is the Almighty God who wants to invade your life with His love and power. This was His intention for the first man, Adam, and it is His intention for you. Richard Bach challenges us with the following statement, "Here is a test to find whether your mission on earth is finished: If you are alive, it isn't." Dear friend, as long as you are breathing the Lord can still breathe on you to fulfill your purpose. Let Him do it!

TWO

THE FIRST BREATH

⚜️ *The Spirit of God has made me,*
And the breath of the Almighty gives me life.

Job 33:4

How would you like to wake up in the morning and find your-self in a beautiful garden paradise with the person who loves you more than any other at your side? What if at that same moment you were also filled with the awareness of why you were born, what you were supposed to do with your life, and where your fu-ture would find you? To top it off, what if you were also given the assurance by the wealthiest person in the world that everything you would ever need would be provided for you? Sound like a dream? This dream was Adam's reality.

At the precise moment the first man, Adam, opened his eyes for the first time, he saw what man was created to see. He heard what man was created to hear. He experienced what man was created to experience. He lived where man was created to live, and he had what man was created to have. Unlike us, Adam did not arrive here to pursue his destiny; he woke up on day one in the middle of his destiny. Seems like an important moment to ponder, doesn't it? Have you ever had one of those moments when it seemed that time became suspended and you found yourself pensively pondering the really serious stuff of life? Thoughts of origins and destinations always seem to visit us in these moments.

7

I remember the day when I first pondered the question, "What was it like for Adam at that first moment when God's breath was breathed upon him?" How powerful it must have been for him to see what he saw, to hear what he heard, and to feel what he felt! When I began thinking about that moment, the revelation started flowing. It was as if someone had flipped a light switch, and pieces of the puzzle started coming together for me. I saw things in a new way and in a different light. It seemed simpler than I had previously realized. I started seeing how much the Scripture tells us that I had not seen before. On that day, I felt like the light bulb of revelation had been turned on in my mind. I could see where I could not see before, and I knew what I did not know before. It all became so much more personal to me.

Often, these light bulb experiences are occasions when God speaks to us. Such an experience can be called a defining moment, an epiphany, an awakening, or a revelation. These are times when our minds get an understanding of what our spirit has been yearning to tell us. This happened to me as I began thinking about Adam's first moment and his first breath.

What would it have been like to be Adam in that first moment of consciousness? What a dynamic miracle it would have been to witness! It was the miracle in which man was made.

> God breathed and boom—
> *Instantaneously, dust became man!*

Wow! Can you imagine seeing a sand pile morphing into a man who gets up and begins walking around? Can you imagine what it would have been like to have been that man? We cannot know everything Adam felt and experienced at that first moment, but I have become convinced that we can know and experience more of it than people might think. I am encouraged by knowing that the God of Adam is the God of me.

We all have this truth in common—*all of us are from the bloodline of Adam*. We can all trace the roots of our family tree back to Adam. If Adam came from God, then so did I. I am not an evolutionist. I am a creationist. As I heard someone once say, "I may have had kinfolks who swung from their necks, but none who swung from their tails." I am not on the upper tier of a progressing evolutionary chain and neither are you! I didn't get to where I am by clawing, fighting, scraping, and surviving my way through the eons of time. Ultimately, all evolutionists will evolve into creationists. They will discover that the missing link they have long sought is called *God*. We are not here because of a big *bang* but because of a big *breath*! The truth is that there are no explanations of the origin of the universe and of man that does not require faith and a string of miracles linked together. To believe in creation is easy for me because I have placed my faith in a God of miracles. I have also tried and tested the truths contained in the Bible in my own life and have found that they are reliable. There is also a long line of voices in history who stand behind me saying, "Amen!"

I am a created being, created in the image of God. That image is not as clear as it ought to be nor as it is going to be; nevertheless, I was placed on this planet with a clear purpose in mind. Discovering that purpose has become eternity's eureka moment in my life. Have you made this discovery? Life is so much more spiritual than most of us have imagined. When our eyes open to this possibility and our hearts become willing, God draws nearer and nearer. He always moves to the place of willingness wherever He sees it. The place of willingness can become the window to eternity where we see God. Because you and I have been beautifully made with eternity in our hearts, there is a part of each of us that longs for God. The world is filled with longing hearts because of this glimmer of eternity in all of our hearts. *He has made everything beautiful in its time. Also He has put eternity in their hearts, except that no one can find out the work that God does from beginning to end* (Ec 3:11).

We cannot understand completely all the work that God does or has done. He is God, and we are not. However, we can know why we are here and why we exist. We are here by Divine choice—not random chance. People were not created to live their lives like rats in a maze trying to figure their way out. We were created to walk with God through life with the certainty that we are here on planet Earth for a purpose. That purpose holds within itself the fulfillment for which you and I have long searched. Do you know what the purpose for your life is?

All of us are God-made. All of us are ultimately related. If we press the rewind button on our heritage, we all end up in Eden at that moment when God created Adam. In a way, we were all there in Eden, inside Adam. The fact that we *are* is because Adam once was. He is the head of the human race—our progenitor. Here's how the Bible describes that awesome first moment when the first man experienced his first breath: *And the LORD God formed man of the dust of the ground, and breathed into his nostrils the breath of life; and man became a living being* (Ge 2:7). Notice, it was the LORD God who formed Adam. He is LORD, and He is God. Get this right, and you are well on your way. You will never truly understand where you came from, why you are here, and where you are going if you leave God out of the equation. If you do not see Him in the beginning of it all, then you are only left with a hopeless situation at the end of it all. Living a God-less life is the shortcut to the destiny-free zone.

THREE

THE HAND THAT MADE ADAM MADE YOU

*But when this work was done, the Divine Artificer still longed for
some creature
which might comprehend the meaning of so vast an achievement,
which might be moved with love at its beauty and smitten with
awe at its grandeur.
When, consequently, all else had been completed (as both Moses
and Timaeus testify),
in the very last place, He bethought Himself of bringing forth man.*

Giovanni Pico della Mirandola,
Oration on the Dignity of Man

Some men boast they are self-made men, but their boasts are not true. The true fountainhead of all blessing is God Himself. As you read this chapter, you will be amazed at how much God was involved in your beginning. God, who is a gardener, took dirt, added to it His breath, and made a man. This shows you how little material the Lord needs to make something extraordinary. It also shows you the creative power of His breath. *And the LORD God formed man of the dust of the ground, and breathed into his nostrils the breath of life; and man became a living being* (Ge 2:7).

The LORD God formed Adam. Like a carpenter cuts out a frame

for a picture and that frame becomes the boundaries of the picture, God formed Adam and surrounded him with boundaries for his life. Adam's body was the frame, and the life within that body was the artistry of God at work. This is the heart of God toward you as well. He wants to form you into the person He created you to be. He wants to work in your life and fashion things so that you will walk in the destiny He has ordained for you. He is a hands-on God, and just as He formed Adam, He desires to form your life as well. He is not aloof, remote, or uninvolved. Jesus taught that God is a Spirit. Therefore, in our true essence we are also spirit. When the spirit leaves the body, the body returns to dust. If you think about it, without the spirit-life of God, we are just dust.

Allow me to elaborate with an illustration often used by preachers, coaches, psychologists, and counselors. Just moments before your conception took place, there were tens of millions of sperm racing to implant themselves into the egg in your mother's body. Only one of those sperm made it, and it was you. You won! You got there first! You are a winner! I remember the awe that flooded my heart when I first heard this illustration through Rev. Johnny Wade Sloan of Hamilton, Ohio. The illustration started me to thinking a little deeper about our origin. Do you realize that a part of you existed before you became the *you* that you now are? I know this sounds confusing, but it is true. A part of you existed prior to the person you now are. It is amazing to think that before you became the person who you now are, there was some preexisting part of you that knew you were headed somewhere. With odds of millions to one, you made it. There was a part of you that knew it was to be a part of something bigger than itself. In other words, the realization of destiny was encoded in a part of you that existed before you became the *you* who you now are.

That little micro part of you had a destination in mind. The destination had to do with another part of you that existed before your conception. That part of you was waiting on something. A racing sperm was looking for a waiting egg. Did you know that every female is born with all the eggs she will ever have? Estimates place the number of eggs present in the female fetus at several million. This makes your birth even more fascinating and staggering. You became *you* as a result of one sperm and one egg coming together. In addition, after the "racing you" came together with the "waiting you," both went on a journey up the fallopian tube to the womb.

Upon arrival, your mother's womb had already been chemically and hormonally alerted to accept the egg. At all other times, the body would have sent antibodies against any intruder to the body, but on the occasion of your conception, everything fell into place. From the moment of your conception, you were accepted. This is all part of the mini-series of miracles that were taking place when you became *you*. An accident? Not at all! Some say life begins at conception. In the strictest sense, it actually begins before conception. The sperm and the egg were both alive before they came together to make the life that would become *you*.

To further state the case of the marvel that became the *you* who you now are, there was only a small window of time that all of this could have taken place. The egg in your mother's body would have only lived 12 to 24 hours outside the ovary had conception not occurred. The sperm that came from your father's body would have lived 48 to 72 hours, if conception had not occurred. To sum it up, one in tens of millions of sperm was able to connect with a single egg from among several million eggs that had been released in a 12- to 24-hour period of time in your mother's body. After they connected, the fertilized egg traveled to the womb where it was able to implant and develop into an embryo which grew into a fetus that 38 weeks later became the newborn known as *you*. A lot of destiny had been put into place before you ever experienced your first breath.

So the two parts of you that existed before you became the you that you now are were characterized by racing and waiting. Does this sound a lot like your life? Racing and waiting. Out of the incredible amount of options and possibilities, you emerged. At any other time, you would not have existed. You are either enormously fortunate due to fate, or you are the direct result of the plans and purposes of God.

That little sperm had, at the most, 72 hours to fulfill its destiny. That little egg had less time, 24 hours at the most. However, the time that they were given was used in a successful way to produce you. This beginning was a snapshot of the life that you are now living. Are you using what you have been given to reach your destiny? There is certainly a part of you that has already experienced success. The average lifespan of a man in the U.S. is now 72 years and for a woman 79 years, according to statistics in the *2001 CIA World Factbook*. How are you using the years you have been given? Are you headed toward your destiny? Is there that part of you that still yearns to join itself to something bigger than you are? In the midst of all the racing and waiting, are you seeing miracles of God's intervention and timing in your life? Can you look back at the part of life you have already lived and see the fingerprints of God upon it? Are you lost? Have you found your way through the maze of life and discovered the hand of God has marked you and led you?

The truth is, God was breathing on your life from the very beginning and maybe even before that. You are not an accident or an afterthought. You are here on purpose. Where you were born was not a mistake. Who your parents are was not a mistake. No, you were born with a destination in mind. Until you understand that ultimate destination, confusion will plague you, and you will continue to alternate between racing and waiting. The dilemma is that you will not know what you are racing *toward*, and you will not know what you are waiting *for*.

To take you backward a little further, think of the fact that the two parts of you that existed before you were also part of two other people—your father and mother. They in turn came from two family lines themselves. As I have mentioned already, it all goes back to Adam and the moment God breathed on him. It was at that moment man was given a body for his spirit. This is really what happens at the moment of conception: a person is given a body for their spirit.

You were created on purpose for a purpose. You are headed somewhere. Since your future is somewhere, somewhere becomes an important place to understand. If you want to do a little theological and philosophical footwork, think on this verse of Scripture from the Book of Jeremiah: *Then the word of the LORD came to me, saying: Before I formed you in the womb I knew you; Before you were born I sanctified you; I ordained you a prophet to the nations* (Je 1:4-5). He had a calling and career before he had a life. He was given a message before he was given a mouth. Like a deeply dug well, this subject goes deeper than my bucket will drop. God is so much more involved in things down here than most people will acknowledge. He knew you before you could be known. He ordained a plan and purpose for you. You can choose to abort that plan, but it is there, and God is ready to help you fulfill it. Because He is God, He has made choices that determine the choices we can make. The secret is to choose the One who has chosen you.

Wow! God knew you before you could be known. What exactly does this mean? Did you exist somewhere else before you existed in your mother's womb? Sure you did! Spirit is eternal. It is not temporal like our fleshly body, it is immaterial and endless. We all had our point of origin in God Himself. I am not saying we are "gods." I am saying in Him we live and move and have our being. I am saying that God is the source of all life, and there would be and can be no life apart from Him. Like it or not (and I suggest you like it), we owe our existence to God. He was making choices about us before we even had the ability to choose. This is the reason we call Him "God!" He has always existed. He has always known what you would be like. You arrived here by no choice of your own, but you do have a choice about where you will go once you have arrived here. God placed you where He did so that you could discover and fulfill His plan for your life.

The Apostle Paul traced humanity's lineage back to one bloodline and wrote that God determined man's pre-appointed times and the boundaries of his dwellings: *And He has made from one blood every nation of men to dwell on all the face of the earth, and has determined their preappointed times and the boundaries of their dwellings* (Ac 17:26).

In other words, before you ever arrived on this planet, God chose when and where you would live. This is the frame of boundaries He placed around you just as He did Adam. He really has a plan for your life! Your life is more than a wooden ball with a letter of the alphabet stamped on it, which rolled out during a divine bingo game. You are here as a result of a deliberate choice and action made by the Almighty God of this universe. In your mother's womb, it was His unseen hand weaving your members together. You were made *by* Him and *for* Him.

Many people reading this book would not have survived their births had they been born in the 18th century. At that time, 300-400 babies out of 1,000 did not survive their births. Now 993 out of 1,000 survive. God determined when you would be born. Praise Him that it was in this hour of human history.

Think of it! You are here because God made you and put you here. You are not an accident, and you most definitely are not a mistake because God does not make mistakes. If He determined the time of your being here, then you did not get here too soon or arrive here too late. You were not made for another time in history; you were made for now! When the day came for you to exit your mother's womb and experience your first breath, God was there. He is the giver of life. You, precious one, are His workmanship. His fingerprints were on your life before you had fingerprints of your own. Your true identity is rooted in God Himself.

FOUR

THE UNIVERSE, THE GARDEN, AND THE WOMB

*The universe is centered on neither the earth
nor the sun. It is centered on God.*

Alfred Noyes

I am a builder by trade. That's right, I am another carpenter turned preacher. I grew up being trained by my Dad to build new houses and remodel older ones. Of course, God is the great builder. He is awesome at building and remodeling, and He isn't limited to houses. Isn't it amazing how He has designed things to function in the universe? Scientists keep discovering that the macro world around us is bigger than they thought and the micro world within us is smaller than they thought.

The discovery of another new planet is becoming more and more commonplace. In 1995, there were only nine known planets in our own solar system. Since that time, through new technology, astronomers and scientists have discovered 145 new planets. I have read that 12 new planets were discovered this year, and one of them is five times the size of Jupiter. Just today, I read in the news where another planet had been discovered, and that Pluto may, in fact, have three moons orbiting around it.[1] Some scientists say this creates problems with some of the theories they have held concerning how planets are formed. They also are saying there are probably many more planets out there than they previously thought.

He is the God of the galaxies. Scientists have not yet been able to determine the number of stars there are in the universe because they keep discovering more universe. There seems to always be another galaxy beyond the last one discovered. Some speculate there are several thousand million billions of stars out there. In our own galaxy, it is estimated that there are over 200 billion stars. Approximately 7,000 stars can be seen from Earth without a telescope, and only 2,000 of them can be seen from any one place at a time. With the most modern telescopes, astronomers are able to see about 70 sextillion stars according to a 2003 study by stargazers at Australian National University.[2] That's 70,000 million million million stars, and that's just the ones that we can see. We are able to see so little of the universe. I checked the HubbleSite Web site (www.hubblesite.org), and there it is stated that the universe "could even extend infinitely in all directions." In other words, whenever they are able to go deeper and see farther, the universe is still expanding. If the universe is expanding at the speed of light, we cannot even think of catching up with it to measure it. Like a cowboy trying to count a stampeding herd of cattle, "It ain't gonna happen."

We are awed by all of this, but for God it took just a few creative declarations and it was done. *By faith we understand that the worlds were framed by the word of God, so that the things which are seen were not made of things which are visible* (He 11:3). As a matter of fact, the universe is still being held together by the Word He spoke: *...and upholding all things by the word of His power...*(He 1:3). If He can do this, what could happen if He spoke into your life? While this is not intended to be a scientific book, there is much relevant information that is meant to remind you how big and awesome God is.

The news of smaller and smaller particles of matter being found is also common. By comparison, a particle of sand to some organisms is like Mt. Everest to us. An atom, not to be confused with Adam, is a really little guy. It is about a tenth of one-millionth of a millimeter wide. However, an atom is composed of even smaller particles. The nucleus of an atom is actually about 100,000 times smaller than the diameter of the atom itself.[3]

Again, with God, it's all in a day's work. For us, we are stupe-
fied by the complexity of it all.

All that God created and established was made to honor and glorify Him. The sun, moon, and stars have done a more consistent job
in this area than humanity has. Yet God made the earth for man to
dwell in. He made the sun to give light by day and the moon to give
light by night. The stars twinkle in wonder and remind us of a
promise that God made to a man named Abraham. The macro-
world and the micro-world are busily performing unceasing duties
as directed by God. Yet God gave us the ability to choose to obey
Him or not. This is intriguing isn't it?

The earth is a very beautiful place that God made for man to inhabit. It is about eight thousand miles wide and has a circumference
of 25,000 miles; that's a lot for one couple to populate. It was created
as a worship sanctuary for man and woman so they could enjoy
each other and God forever. To top all of this, God created a *master
suite* called the Garden of Eden. It was the room of pleasure inside
the big house called Earth that Father God built for His kids.

According to the 1928 Edition of Webster's Dictionary, the word
woman comes from combining the two words, "womb" and "man."
In other words, a woman is a man with a womb. Other dictionaries
define it as being the wife of a man. The Genesis account tells us she
was called woman because she was taken out of man: *And Adam
said: "This is now bone of my bones and flesh of my flesh; she shall be
called Woman, because she was taken out of Man"* (Ge 2:23).

This is a play on the two Hebrew words, *ishah* (literally, "of
man") and *ish* (man). Although the woman came from the man, she
was more than a man. She had the ability to bear children. She was
given a womb. One wise guy jokingly said, "When Adam saw Eve,
he said, 'Whoa! Man!'" But Genesis reveals to us that Adam saw
Eve and declared, "Bone of my bones and flesh of my flesh." In
other words, "She's like me, she came out of me."

I have already described in this chapter how God created the
universe and how it became a dwelling place for the earth. He created the earth as the special dwelling place for man. Then He created Eden as a special garden on Earth for man and woman to live
forever in pleasure with God.

I want to propose to you that God created the womb within
woman as a place where He could continue to manifest His creative
activity. I understand He rested on the seventh day declaring all

that He had created as good and very good. However, there is no doubt that God continues to manifest His creative power at different times and in different ways throughout the biblical record, whether it's parting the sea for Moses, multiplying the loaves for Jesus, or healing the cripple for Peter. In the womb of a woman, we discover some of God's most creative activity. His hand actually weaved you together in your mother's womb:

> *For You formed my inward parts;*
> *You covered me in my mother's womb.*
> *I will praise You, for I am fearfully* and *wonderfully made;*
> *Marvelous are Your works,*
> *And* that *my soul knows very well.*
> *My frame was not hidden from You,*
> *When I was made in secret,*
> *And* skillfully *wrought in the lowest parts of the earth.*
> *Your eyes saw my substance, being yet unformed.*
> *And in Your book they all were written,*
> *The days fashioned for me,*
> *When* as yet there were *none of them.*
> *How precious also are Your thoughts to me, O God!*
> *How great is the sum of them!*
> *If I should count them, they would be more in number than the sand;*
> *When I awake, I am still with You.*
>
> Psalm 139:13-18

As I stated in the last chapter, at the time of your conception and development, the purposes of God resulted in you. Let's look biblically at some of the things God did for you while you were in your mother's womb. With the help of the *The Complete Word Study Dictionary: Old Testament,* we will see just how much God was involved in bringing you into this earth to fulfill His purposes. The following descriptions speak to us about God's work in the womb of woman.

He formed your inward parts.

The word *formed* means "to form" but has the connotation of bought, acquired, redeemed, and possessed. We experience being born again because of the redemptive blood of Jesus Christ that was shed for us. But this is true not only for the second birth but for the first birth as well. Adam and Eve never would have had children if God had not covered them with His mercy and grace. He took the skins of an animal and covered them in their nakedness before they were driven out of the garden into the earth to live their lives. Shortly after this, we read that Eve bore a son. You and I never would have been born had it not been for the redemptive heart of God. Both our first birth (physical) and second birth (spiritual) are rooted in the redemptive purposes of God. You were formed in your mother's womb by the redemptive hand of God.

He covered you in your mother's womb.

The word *covered* means "to cover, hide, shield, and protect something." It is the word used of the cherubim's wings covering the lid of the Ark of the Covenant. While you were in your mother's womb, God covered and shielded you. This is another reason why abortion is so wrong. Until recent years, the child in the womb has been protected by law. Unfortunately that has changed, and the womb where the hand of God does such beautiful creative work is now vulnerable to the dangerous hand of man. The womb is the place where the creative work of God continues to express itself. To intrude and stop this beautiful work of God opposes the work that God is doing in the womb. The word also has a connotation of weaving. God was actually weaving your life and destiny together as you developed inside your mother's womb.

He made you fearfully and wonderfully.

The phrase *fearfully and wonderfully made* means "to be distinct, separate, set apart, different." You always knew it, didn't you? You are different, but so are all the rest of us. Snowflakes don't have an edge on any of us. God had something very distinct in mind when He made you, and His intentions were good. You have been set apart by His hand. His creative genius was at work making you for the special purposes He ordained for your life.

You were a marvelous work.

Marvelous means "to do something wonderful, extraordinary, or difficult." Not only are you different, but you are extraordinary and complicated. The word "work" has the idea of workmanship. How amazing it is to realize that the Master Craftsman of the universe

made something marvelous, and it was you. You really are the result of the miraculous activity of God. When a person becomes a
Christian, he is called the workmanship of God. But in reality, every
person begins the journey into this life as the workmanship of God.
We experience it in the natural when we are given life. Then we experience it in the spiritual when we are saved and given eternal life.

Your frame was not hidden from Him.

The word *frame* refers to the strength and substance that you were
given. Your strength and might were not concealed or hidden from
God. He was actually the supplier of the strength you were given in
the womb. As you grew, God kept His eyes on you. You were never
hidden from Him. You were not "something" taking place outside
His knowledge or will. When you were born, God did not jump in
surprise that you appeared on the earth's scene. He did not ask,
"Where did you come from?" As you exerted your strength making
the journey through the womb of your mother, God saw it all and
He was glad.

You were made in secret.

The word *made* used here is the same word found in the creation account in Genesis. God really does continue His creative activity in
the womb. You are made by God and made in the image of God.
The term *secret* speaks of a secret hiding place. When God made the
first person, Adam, He was alone in the Garden of Eden. In a similar way, in the womb, God continues to work creatively unseen by
anyone else. Another powerful thought to consider is that Christians are called to meet God in the secret place. In Psalm 91, we are
told to dwell in the secret place of the Most High God. Interestingly,
our life journey in this world began in our mother's womb where
God was meeting with us in the secret place. Yes, David said in
Psalm 51, *in sin my mother conceived me.* But isn't it true that everyone since Adam and Eve who has come to know God did so as a
sinner? If the Lord was unwilling to work with sinners, He would
have no one to work with at all!

You were skillfully wrought.

Skillfully wrought means "to embroider, to weave, to do needlework." In
one of its forms, it designates a person skilled in doing all kinds of em-

broidery work. When I was a little boy, my grandmother would often make quilts while baby-sitting me. A quilt frame hung from the ceiling on her covered back porch. Most of the time fabric was stretched out on it, and a quilt was in process. I remember, as a five year old, spending hours sitting under the quilt frame as she worked. Thursdays were always special. That was the day the garbage truck dumped the scraps and discarded spools from the sewing plant in town. The county dump was just a couple of miles from my grandmother's house. She would always get someone to drive us there, and we would rummage through the scraps of material that Mama Lawrence used to make her quilts. She would lay her hand-made patterns on the scraps and cut out the shapes she desired. Doggies, kitties, ducks, and flowers seemed to be her favorites. She would then begin sewing them onto the top of squares of other colored fabric. Then she attached them and made a beautiful quilt. I still have the one she made for me when I was being quilted together in my mother's womb.

Your unformed substance was seen by Him.

The unformed substance in question here is the fetus or embryo. The actual meaning of the word is "the embryonic child in the womb." The Scripture bears witness in this verse that God saw you when you were being formed in your mother's womb. He saw you throughout the whole process of your development and birth. A little later in this chapter you are going to see just how much God has His attention on you.

You were written about in His book.

The psalmist also tells us (139:16) that God has a book that records everything about you as well as the days you would live. We are often encouraged to journal our thoughts about God, but it's neat to think that God has a book that journals His thoughts and plans about us. The Bible mentions in different places that there are books that contain information about us. The Lamb's Book of Life will show who has trusted Jesus to save them. The books described in Revelation 20 contain all the deeds people performed on Earth who did not trust Jesus for their salvation. The psalmist mentions a book containing information about the developing child. The Hebrew word for book, *safer*, has great nuances of meaning. The basic meaning of the word is "a document, a book, a scroll." It is used to speak of a proof or purchase deed. God has an owner's certificate with your name on it. His divine right is rooted in the fact that He is your creator, but you also have been purchased with the blood of Jesus. The next time the devil is giving you trouble, remind him that you belong to God, the blood of Jesus is the price of purchase, and in God's book there is the proof of purchase.

Another powerful way *safer* is used is in referring to a book in which things were written for a need in the future. This is a great encouragement to the child of God. Even before you were born, God was recording in a book everything that you would need in the future. Remember, because God is God, He knows everything, even your future. Isn't it awesome that everything you will need to fulfill God's purposes and plan for your life is already authorized in Heaven? When you are pursuing that plan and those purposes and simply ask in faith for whatever you need, it is given to you.

Safer is also used in reference to a genealogical record. This means that God not only has provided for our own lives but for our whole family line. Recently, my wife was doing some genealogical research. She discovered a Web site that contained all kinds of information. They had records of passenger lists of people who sailed from Europe to America. They had immigration records for the early years of our nation. They had Civil War records. There were many other databases to find relatives by last names. People are interested in their roots. We may often be confused about how our family tree branches out. However, one of God's books contains information about you and me and all our family lines.

Basically, this precious book contains information about your destiny. Predestination is a big, twelve-cylinder, theological word. I do not pretend to be able to understand or explain it. I do suggest that you look at it in a different way than you may have before. Let's break it down. Predestination, a destination ahead of time, or a destiny ahead of time. In simple terms, the Lord has chosen a destiny ahead of time for each of us. Before we were formed in our mothers' wombs, God had a plan of destiny for you and me. That plan may very well be laid out in the book mentioned in Psalm 139. With this in mind, read a familiar passage of Scripture: *And we know that all things work together for good to those who love God, to those who are the called according to His purpose. For whom He foreknew, He also predestined to be conformed to the image of His Son, that He might be the firstborn among many brethren* (Ro 8:28-29). God has promised to those who choose to love Him and those who have answered the call to His purpose that He will work all things together for good. He will work things together in a way that our lives will intersect with His purposes and the result is that we will be like Jesus. Notice also that Paul refers to the fact that God foreknew; therefore, He predestined. The destiny He planned was that, in addition to His only begotten Son, there would be many that would become brethren to His Son. Again, we see that Father wants sons and daughters, and He wants them to all carry the character of His Son Jesus. In the fourth century A.D., Saint Athanasius stated, "He became what we are that He might make us what He is." Your destiny cannot be accomplished apart from Jesus Christ. Your true destiny involves becoming like Jesus. Father had all of it planned even before you began development in your mother's womb.

Your days were fashioned before you were ever born.

This is another powerful truth. He fashioned your days before you were ever born. The key is to live each day with the knowledge that God has a plan for you for that day. Just like the next piece of pattern sewn to the quilt on my grandmother's frame, life begins to blossom, to take shape, and to feel full when it is lived in alignment with God's purposes. We should declare Psalm 118:24 over each day as we awaken: *This is the day the LORD has made; We will rejoice and be glad in it* (Ps 118:24). Knowing that the Lord has made this day gives us the assurance of His presence and power to fulfill His purposes for this day that He has fashioned and made for us to live.

His thoughts about you are precious.

How precious also are Your thoughts to me, O God! How great is the sum of them!

Psalm 139:17

The word *precious* is a verb meaning "to esteem, to be valuable, to be costly." It has the idea of being highly valuable, worthy. In other words, Father God sees you as highly valuable. The word is sometimes used in conjunction with the idea of redemption. When Father sees you, He sees a person He loves so much that He was willing to give His only begotten Son to die for you. He gave heaven's greatest treasure to redeem you—the precious blood of

His own dear Son. He certainly thinks you are worth a lot. Want to know your value? Look at the price God paid for you!

His thoughts toward you are innumerable.

How precious also are Your thoughts to me, O God! How great is the sum of them! If I should count them, they would be more in number than the sand; When I awake, I am still with You.

Psalm 139:17-18

As of the date of this writing, the world's fastest supercomputer is housed in Livermore, California, at the Lawrence Livermore National Laboratory.[4] Built at the cost of $100 million, this IBM-based computer was clocked at a sustained speed of 135.3 teraflops. A teraflop is the speed of a computer that can perform one trillion calculations per second. The owners of the computer say that the peak speed of the computer is around 360 teraflops. Now let's do some comparison and application of these facts.

We are told the current population on Earth is about six billion people. For the sake of illustration, we will allow each person to represent one calculation on the world's fastest supercomputer. This means that, at its sustained speed, the world's current fastest supercomputer could compute every person on the planet 22,500 times per second. At its peak speed it could process each person almost 60,000 times per second. Here's the point. If a computer made by the mind of man can process this much information every second (and God could do at least as much as man can do), then God can think of you as an individual at least 60,000 times every second while doing the same thing for every other person on the planet at the same time. Back in the nineties, I remember hearing a cassette tape by James Ryle, who was teaching on God's grace. He shared about the speed a quartz crystal vibrates when energy passes through it. At that time, his conclusion was that at the very least God could think of every person on earth several times every second. His teaching stirred me to realize how great God really is. We all accept what man has been able to do; therefore, we should conclude that God can do more. The discovery of new technology continually expands our thinking of how much man can do. God can do beyond what man can ever imagine doing. We must remove the limitations we have imposed on the greatness of our God.

Computer gurus in Japan and the U.S. are racing for the next world's fastest supercomputer.[5] Before 2010 they will have computers that will operate about ten times faster than the current peak speeds. This means that a man-made computer will be able to calculate at 3 to 4 petaflops. A petaflop is the equivalent of 1,000 teraflops per second. To simplify, this would be about 4,000 teraflops. If every person on the globe was a single calculation, all six billion people could be calculated over 600,000 times per second. If we are willing to give God the same amount of mental power, then He is able to think about you at least 600,000 times per second while doing the same for every other person on the globe. But God is able to do far more than man could ever conceive of doing. In addition, His thoughts toward you are precious. Read the following verses that tell you more about God's thoughts toward you:

> Many, O LORD my God, are Your wonderful works
> Which You have done;
> And Your thoughts toward us
> Cannot be recounted to You in order;
> If I would declare and speak of them,
> They are more than can be numbered.
>
> Psalm 40:5

> For I know the thoughts that I think toward you, says the LORD, thoughts of peace and not of evil, to give you a future and a hope.
>
> Jeremiah 29:11

How incredible that the God who made the universe and stretched out the skies is thinking about you every moment of every day. He was thinking about you when He made the universe for you to enjoy. He was thinking about you when He made the earth for you to inhabit. He was thinking about you when you were developing in your mother's womb. He is thinking about you right now at the rate of at least 600,000 times per second. Wow! He can provide you His undivided attention while He does the same for me and every other breathing person on the planet. With this in mind, it is easy to see how God can hear all our prayers without being confused. It is easy for God to stay up to the second on everything going on in your life and to orchestrate all things together for good in your life. His thoughts and His purposes are very intertwined, but He never gets tangled up when it comes to you. Because He knows all that is going on in every life on the globe, He is able to work it all together for good. He promises to do this for all those who love Him. You cannot know everything God thinks, but you can know He thinks about you. He thinks a lot *about* you, and He thinks a lot *of* you.

The mystery of it all is "Why?" The psalmist also was somewhat mystified by this:

> *When I consider Your heavens, the work of Your fingers,*
> *The moon and the stars, which You have ordained,*
> *What is man that You are mindful of him,*
> *And the son of man that You visit him?*
> *For You have made him a little lower than the angels,*
> *And You have crowned him with glory and honor.*

Psalm 8:3-5

When the psalmist looked up at the heavens and saw all that God had made, he wondered why God would allow His mind to be centered on man. In addition, he was at a loss to understand why the Lord would visit and fellowship with man. To top it off, he was astounded that God would make man just below Himself. The word "angels" in verse five is the Hebrew word *Elohim* which means "God." It is staggering when you look at the majesty and grandeur of God and realize that He has chosen to focus His loving attention on you and me.

God was as involved in creating you as He was in creating Adam. With this in mind, let's go back to that first moment in Adam's life when the breath of God brought him up from the dust. This is the moment Divinity touched dust and produced a destiny. There's more to this mystery, so keep reading. The best is yet to come!

FIVE

YOUR DESTINY IS IN YOUR SPIRITUAL DNA

You got to be careful if you don't know where you're going,
because you might not get there.

Yogi Berra

D o you know what you want in life? Most people don't. Once
you know what you want, you have to decide how much you
want it. The degree of your desire will determine the level of passion that will be present for you to obtain whatever it is you want.
I think it is important to know what you want. It is even more important that you want the right things. Too often, we allow circumstances to do the choosing for us. There is a plan for your life that
has been ordained by God Himself. Our wanting must be in alignment with His wanting. The two greatest questions with which human beings have always grappled are, "Where did I come from?"
and "Why am I here?" Through the ages, philosophers have batted
their speculations about these questions back and forth across their
intellectual podiums of debate. World religions have weighed in to
supply their answers. In the myriad of opinions struggling for
prominence, there can be only one right answer. Since we were not
here first, it seems reasonable to allow the One who was here first
to explain it to us. Until your ears hear the truth from the One who
is the Truth, you will always feel as though you are chasing some-

29

thing you will never catch. That which would fulfill your yearning heart will always seem to elude you, leaving you numb and on the run. Most people have a dream that tells them there is more than they are experiencing. We have to learn to mix intention with our dreams to see them come true. The people who see their dreams come true can still end up empty if it has been all sweat and no spirit. Only the sweet nectar of heaven can satisfy the part of you that truly yearns for destiny. Everything else is just like a good dessert, wonderful until you're through with it. The temporary will never fill the place made for the eternal. To try to replace the eternal with the temporal is an affront to who you really are and to the One who made you.

There has been enough of man trying to replace God's wisdom with his ignorance. I like what D.L. Moody had to say about the worldview of a Christian. "The Christian on his knees sees more than the philosopher on tiptoe." God is not looking for someone to serve Him in an advisory capacity. Just this week, I read of a "famed" atheist who has now been scientifically convinced that there is a God.[6]

He remains unwilling to believe this "God" cares about him. At least he and others like him are realizing the facts point us toward a creator of all things. Man's desire to exalt himself above God goes all the way back to Eden when the serpent spit his poison on Adam and Eve. Before the days of creation, Lucifer also tried to exalt himself above God. He wanted the loot, but he got the boot. This always happens when we turn in our application for God's job. This reminds me of the following little fable I once heard.

One day a group of scientists got together and decided that man had developed so much intelligence that he no longer needed God. So they picked one scientist to go inform God that they were done with Him. The scientist went to God and said, "God, we've decided that we no longer need you. We can now clone people and do many miraculous things, so why don't you just get lost."

God listened very patiently and kindly to the man. When the scientist was finished talking, God said, "Very well, how about this, let's say we have a man-making contest." To which the scientist replied, "OK, great!" But, God added, "We're going to do this just like I did back in the old days with Adam." The scientist said, "Sure, no problem," and proceeded to bend over and grab a handful of dirt. God just looked at him and said, "No! You make your own dirt!"[7]

How absurd to think that everything that exists just happened! Man is seen as the top of the chain, but who made the chain? God made it happen, and He has always existed. Science can study the creation, but it cannot replace the Creator. Exalting science over Scripture is foolish and unwise. This sentiment was evidenced in 1963 by Dr. Martin Luther King, Jr.: "Our scientific power has outrun our spiritual power. We have guided missiles and misguided men."[8] Science has helped us in many ways to understand ourselves and our world. However, to use it to eliminate the moral code of conduct set forth by our Creator sets humanity on a dangerous course. Abraham Lincoln realized that the condition of the world could confuse people in their belief about God. He encouraged people to look above for the inspiration they needed. He said, "I can see how it might be possible for a man to look down upon the earth and be an atheist, but I cannot conceive how he could look up into the heavens and say there is no God."

The scientific complexities of man are fascinating. Your physical body is made of millions upon millions of strands of DNA. Some of the markers in your DNA are unique to you. The DNA molecule is a double helix, shaped like a twisted ladder. It is found in the core of who you are. Your body's basic building blocks are composed of DNA. The genetic information that is stored on the 46 chromosomes at the center of each human cell is called the human genome. Amazingly, all of your ancestral characteristics are stored and encoded within you. Some are more active than others are. Some characteristics dominate the other characteristics. You are the result of factors that existed before *you* did.

There is even a new field of study called anthrogenealogy where microbiology and genetics are used to study a person's ancestral lineage beyond the available historical records of a person's family line. The shapes and characteristics that form the human body are carried from one generation to the next. All the little nuances that make each of us a little different are carried and expressed through the DNA genetic structure. If this is true of the physical part of you, would it be too far-fetched to think it is true of the soulish and spiritual part of you? We all agree that our hair color, eye color, and stature came from our dad and mom. Could it be that our acceptance of God or resistance to God has been affected by our family line as well? Both genetic and environmental factors have contributed to what you believe about God. One of the great opportu-

nities of parenting is to be able to teach children that they were created by God with a purpose that is bigger than they are. In the Old
Testament, Moses commanded the people to keep God's laws and
to teach it to their children. In this way, the Scriptures would be in-
culcated into their lives and family lines. What parents do in rela-
tion to God certainly affects their children's mindset toward God.

Life is movement. We are living toward something. Otherwise,
you are left with a temporal, meaningless existence. The Bible
teaches us that we are headed toward where we came from. As the
present becomes history and we step into tomorrow's future, we
will meet God face to face. Whether you will want to flee from Him
or cling to Him at that moment is being determined right now. The
way you are living now is programming you for eternity. If you are
not devoted to Him now, you will not know devotion to Him then.
We will all bow before Him. Whether you bow and remain with
Him, or bow and are removed from Him, is determined by the
choices of your heart in the here and now. Your choices will, to some
degree, influence the next generation of your family line.

Like trying to describe the beauty of a Hawaiian sunset to someone who has never seen one, words cannot express how incredibly
life-changing it is when the human heart has been touched by the
love of God. You have to experience it to know its wonders! You
were made to experience His love. I believe that deep inside your
DNA there is a distant memory of the breath of God being breathed
upon your great, great, great, great, etc., grandfather, Adam. Closer
to where you are now, you may have had ancestors who felt the
breath of God sweeping into their lives. The fact that you are reading this book may be linked to a prayer prayed by a relative of a
prior generation. Their pursuit of God may have sowed the seed for
your pursuit of God. Isn't it interesting to consider that your great-
grandmother's prayer still carries weight in heaven? I believe the
Bible teaches us that generational negatives and generational posi-
tives can be passed on to us through our family lineage.

You and I can trace our heritage back to the moment of creation
when God transformed dust into man. The truths and events surrounding this first moment also give us further glimpses of why we
are here. This is the place where we find our history and our destiny. Where we came from and where we are supposed to go are all
to be discovered in the first moments of human history.

When Adam's eyes opened in that first moment of time, He was face to face with his destiny. He looked into the face of God with the instantaneous knowledge that He belonged to God. At that moment, he did not struggle with the question, "Why do I exist?" That question was settled with the first beat of his heart. He belonged to God. Everything he would ever need was to be found in the face he was beholding. When we have this experience, we also cease our struggle. Our minds search for reason; God is all wisdom. Our hearts search for love; God is love. Our eyes search for light; God is light. Everything that we search for is to be found in Him. When you discover this, it is awesome!

The bottom line is that when a human receives revelation from the Divine, the human has the opportunity to be forever changed. It must be this way. The lesser must give way to the greater. Man, who is not God, can never replace the knowledge that he came from God with anything else that will ever completely satisfy him. But we have tried!

When you open your Bible to its first pages, you read about the creation of the world and the creation of man. The first book of the Bible is called Genesis. *Genesis* means 'beginning.' Genesis is the book of beginnings. The first words in the first book are, *In the beginning God created the heavens and the earth.* The existence of God is assumed. It is the safest assumption a person could ever make.

In the next verse, you find the first mention of the Spirit of God. He is hovering, literally brooding, fluttering like a hummingbird, over the face of the deep. The Bible says that the earth was formless and empty. While the Holy Spirit hovered over a formless and empty Earth, God began speaking. This is what I refer to as the principle of the *Stirring Spirit and the Spoken Word*. All through the Bible, we see God doing amazing things through the movement of His Spirit and the declaration of His Word. When God spoke His Word into what His Spirit was doing, it resulted in dynamic, explosive, and creative results. The first mention of the release of His Word into the realm of the earth brought light. The release of His Word still brings light. When we learn to identify where the Holy Spirit is moving and speak God's word into what His Spirit is doing, we also get dynamic, powerful results.

What God created shows us His heart. You can study how God moved in the first moments of creative history and discover the motivations of His heart. By discerning what He wanted, His original intentions, you can then align your life with those intentions and step into your destiny. Knowing why you were created is a very important question. If you answer this question correctly and pursue the truth of that answer, you will find yourself a blessed person indeed. You will have found the supreme goal of living. You will have found the pleasure of the heart of Almighty God, and you will have found the reason for your very existence. Ultimate fulfillment is the reward of this grand discovery. We need to see the heart of God in His original intentions.

What you will learn as we look into Adam and Eve's first days together will give you confident insight into the last days. The Book of Beginnings reveals to us the Book of Endings. Yes, our history is recorded in the Book of Genesis, but our destiny is recorded in the Book of the Revelation.

How God created *what* He created is very important. In creation, we see God in action. People's actions reveal their hearts. Their behavior paints a picture of what they believe. As we look at what God did and how He did it, we gain a deeper understanding of what He was after in creating what He created. Let me share one example of what I am trying to express to you out of the following passage: *The earth was without form, and void; and darkness* was *on the face of the deep. And the Spirit of God was hovering over the face of the waters* (Ge 1:2).

The earth was formless. It was void. The word "void," as used here, means empty. The earth was empty. What did God do? As you read on through the following verses, you discover that God began filling that which was empty. The expanse of the cosmos was empty. What did He do? He filled it with the sun, moon, stars, planets, and galaxies. The sky was empty. What did He do? He filled the sky with birds that would fly. The vast sea was empty. What did He do? He filled it with fish and underwater creatures. The landscape was barren and empty. What did He do? He filled it with all manner of living beasts and creeping things. The ground was empty. What did He do? He caused it to be filled with grass, herbs, plants, and fruit-bearing trees.

He filled the galaxies; He filled the skies; He filled the sea; He filled the land; He filled the ground. To top it all off, He took dust from the ground and formed it into the shape of a man. He then filled man with Himself. That's right; He filled man with His very own breath of life. As God's breath became Adam's first breath, Adam awakened as a perfect man in a perfect place with a perfect life before a perfect God. This is the stuff that makes paradise—paradise!

Adam was the pinnacle of God's creative activity. Adam was also the purpose for the rest of God's creative activity. Everything else God had created through those first days was to prepare a living place for the pinnacle of His creative activity—man. The whole earth was formless and empty, and God shaped it and filled it. Why? Because He knew He would be shaping a man, forming him, and then filling that man with His own likeness. He knew He would make a woman from the man, and the two of them would multiply. He knew they would need a home.

He even gave Adam and Eve dominion over all the rest of creation. It was to be theirs to enjoy. He wanted a place for His children to live with Him. He still wants the same thing with you! This is the reason our heart doesn't find its home until we come home to God.

It didn't take long for the first man to leave his home, and the rest of the Bible is the story of a loving Father waiting for His sons and daughters to come home. As a matter of fact, one of the greatest stories Jesus ever told was about a father waiting on a prodigal son to come home. When that son finally came home, there was quite a celebration. Why? There is no place like home. If you are struggling in a dark place living a life that is not in relationship with God, let me remind you that a loving Heavenly Father has left a light on for you and He's peeking out the window waiting on you. He wants you to come home.

SIX

UNDERSTANDING YOUR SPIRITUAL DNA

I believe in Christianity as I believe that the sun has risen:
not only because I see it,
but because by it I see everything else.

C. S. Lewis

God filled man with Himself. This is an intoxicating thought, but this is what we find when we read the account of God creating Adam. *And the LORD God formed man of the dust of the ground, and breathed into his nostrils the breath of life; and man became a living being* (Ge 2:7). God breathed on that dirt and that lump of dirt became animated, filled with the very life of God. He had created the animals, but it would be a man-shaped mound of dust that He breathed into who would bear His image in the earth. When God's breath entered that mound of dust, Adam came alive unto God.

I started imagining, "What would it have been like to have been Adam in that first moment of awareness? What was that first moment of consciousness like?" The very moment that the fresh moist breath of God touched those compacted particles of dirt, an astounding miracle took place. The first human being woke up to say "Hello" to his Creator.

Think of it—the first thing Adam saw was the *face* of God. The first voice Adam heard was the *voice* of God. The first awareness

37

Adam ever experienced was of the *presence* of God. The first emotion that he felt was of the *love* of God. Adam was made to see God's face, hear God's voice, live in God's presence, and receive God's love.

All of us exist for the same reason. As mentioned previously, deep inside our DNA, we all carry the quest for God. It has become distorted by sin; but nonetheless, it still lingers deep inside us. Deep calls unto deep. This means if there is a desire that arises out of us, then there is a corresponding reality to answer that desire. This is true of godly and ungodly desires. The desire to know God is deep in our DNA. It goes all the way back—trace the trail—all the way back to the lungs of Adam when God breathed life into him.

God put Adam in a place called Eden. Eden means "pleasure." He wanted His son Adam to experience communion with Him. This communion already existed in God. God experiences a wonderful communion within Himself. This is the unity of the Trinity— God the Father, God the Son, and God the Holy Spirit. God wanted to expand that fellowship. It pleased God to create man. He created a human son. His son was given a physical body and had the Spirit of God living inside of him. He called him Adam. He breathed His life into him—made him in His image. He also made a wife for him, a helpmate. He placed them in the Garden of Eden. They began their lives in the presence of God.

The presence of God was what made it such a joy-filled, pleasurable place. The Bible says, *You will show me the path of life; In Your presence is fullness of joy; At Your right hand are pleasures forevermore* (Ps 16:11). Often people become depressed because they do not sense the presence of God in their lives. Knowing God loves you and is with you enables you to experience joy in life.

There is no pleasure to be found which can compare to the pleasure of being in the presence of God. Adam and you were made to live in the presence of God. We were all made to live in His presence. In fact, you really cannot *live* without it. God is a spirit. Man was made in God's image. Therefore, man in his true essence is spirit. So, you are a spirit. You are a spirit being who inhabits a body.

God also gave man a soul. The spirit and soul are very closely related since they are both invisible and intangible. Many times in the Bible, soul and spirit are seen as one. In simple terms, soul and spirit are the unseen parts of you, while the body is the seen part of you. To be accurate, there is a difference between the soul and spirit (1 Th 5:23). The soul is that inside part of you that makes you different from other people. It is your uniqueness. For example, twins may look alike on the outside, but they are different on the inside. Our soul is the part of us that makes us individuals. It is in our soul that we make choices. Those choices will lead us toward or separate us from God and His plans for our lives. Our soul is made up of our mind, emotions, affections, will, reason, imagination, and personality. The soul is also the seat of our senses and our appetites. It is obvious there is an unseen part of you, which is the "real" you. For example, you can lose your mind but still have a brain. The brain is just the physical part of you that the mind uses to function. Really, it is your brain that you lose; therefore, your mind does not have a way to express itself through your body. Your spirit and soul are able to communicate to the external world around you through your body.

Your body is just a home for your spirit. The earth is just a home for your body. In other words, God, who is a Spirit, created you as a spirit with a soul. He put you in a body so that you could live on the earth, which also belongs to Him. The true you is your spirit. Since God who made you is eternal, then you are eternal in your spirit. The forever part of you is another facet of the image of God in you. He really has put eternity in your heart!

I once heard Dr. Adrian Rogers of Memphis, Tennessee, preach about the spirit, soul, and body. I love the way he described their functions. He taught that when your body is functioning the way God made it to, you are healthy. When your soul is rightly related to God, you are happy. When your spirit is right with God, you are holy. I like that description, don't you? Healthy, happy, and holy describe Adam's condition after God breathed into him the breath of life.

It is in your spirit that you can experience communion with God's Spirit. When you do not have a relationship with God, His Spirit is not dwelling in your spirit. Paul wrote that it is when God's Spirit bears witness with your spirit that you can know you belong to God (Ro 8:16). God wants you to come in spirit to Him as your Father and worship Him. *But the hour is coming, and now is, when the true worshipers will worship the Father in spirit and truth; for the Father is seeking such to worship Him. God is Spirit, and those who worship Him must worship in spirit and truth* (Jo 4:23-24).

With all this in mind, you can begin to see it is vital that we learn about the Spirit of God. We also must learn how to live life through our spirit by being led by His Spirit. Father God wants us to walk and talk with Him and know that He wants to walk and talk to us. Because He is Spirit and we are spirit, we need to expect things to happen in the Spirit. I encourage you to realize that the Scriptures were inspired by the Spirit of God and contain the truth about who God is and who man is. A mechanic can tell you how your car engine operates. An electrician can tell you how your house is wired. A doctor can tell you about the physical aspects of your being. But you need someone who understands the realm of the spirit to help you understand who you are as a Spirit. The expert on the spirit is the Spirit of God.

SECTION TWO

FATHER'S HEART
TOWARD YOU

SEVEN

THE FATHER'S FIRST BREATH

What is our relationship to God? . . .
The position that we stand in to Him is
that of a son. Adam is the father of our bodies,
and God is the father of our spirits.

John Taylor

Did you know that the Bible calls "Adam," a son of God? Luke traces the genealogy of Jesus through His legal earthly father, Joseph, all the way back to Adam. ...The son *of Enosh*, the son *of Seth*, the son *of Adam*, the son *of God* (Lk 3:38). Adam is called "the son of God." Literally, Luke wrote "Adam of God." Adam came from God in the same sense that Issac came from Abraham and Abel came from Adam. This is obvious. If Adam did not come from God, then where did he come from? Luke's purpose is to show lineage and origin. As Issac proceeded from Abraham, so Adam proceeded from God. Adam came from God. This is theologically unquestionable if you stick to the biblical account. To arrive at a different conclusion, you must adopt a competing theory of his coming into existence. Adam had his origin from God. God is viewed to be Adam's Father. I am not saying that Adam was equal to Jesus. He was not "the only begotten" son of God but was a child of God in the same sense that we by the new birth are "children" of

God (Jo 1:12). He was a man full of God's spirit. Whatever the basis of relationship between Adam and God was before the fall, it was pure and perfect and unhindered. I do not think Luke included the "Adam of God" phrase to take away from Jesus, but to show that man himself was a special creative work of God to the degree that God came after him to redeem him. And He is still pursuing that relationship with mankind. Please note what the notable Greek scholar A.T. Roberson says about this:

It is in harmony with Pauline universality (Plummer) that Luke carries the genealogy back to Adam and does not stop with Abraham. It is not clear why Luke adds "the Son of God" after Adam (Luke 3:38). Certainly he does not mean that Jesus is the Son of God only in the sense that Adam is. Possibly he wishes to dispose of the heathen myths about the origin of man and to show that God is the Creator of the whole human race, Father of all people in that sense. No mere animal origin of man is in harmony with this conception.[9]

To what degree did Adam come from God is the next question? Creatively he came from God just as the sun, moon, and stars. But Adam also possessed something the rest of creation did not—the image of God within him. The animals had breath but not image. Adam was made to relate to God as one who bore His likeness. Adam related to God as the One from whom he came. Jesus was God becoming a man. Adam was a man who came from God. The incarnation is the act of God becoming a man and living among humanity to redeem and restore him. The restoration of man places him back in right relationship with God as God originally intended. I believe we do God and Adam injustice when we limit their relationship to the single act of creation. We need to see the passion in the heart of God to create someone who had His image—that someone to whom He could show His love. We are told early in Genesis that Adam and God communed together in the Garden. They talked and related to one another. This was in God's heart toward Adam before He ever breathed him into being. It is what He is after with you as well. When God created Adam, He became Father to the entire human race. This is what He wanted and still wants. He wants to have sons and daughters who will bear His image and reflect His glory all across the earth. In the deepest essence of our being, there is a hunger to experience the Father love of God. This incredible love is the true motive of life. Without it, we miss the mark. When Adam opened his eyes, he saw his Father, God.

Last year, I taught the congregation which I pastor about the forerunner anointing. I had been preparing that particular week to teach them how God pours out the spirit of Elijah on fathers and children to turn their hearts toward one another. The last two verses in the Old Testament state, *Behold, I will send you Elijah the prophet Before the coming of the great and dreadful day of the* LORD. *And he will turn The hearts of the fathers to the children, And the hearts of the children to their fathers, Lest I come and strike the earth with a curse* (Mal 4:5-6).

When Sunday morning came, I awakened about 4:30 a.m. It was one of those times that I just snapped awake. I have learned that when this happens, it is often the Lord wanting to communicate something to me. As I lay there waiting before the Lord, I heard what I believe was His still, small voice saying, "I want you to find the first occurrence of the word 'Father' in the Bible and listen to it."

I was excited to have been given this directive. I immediately got up and headed to my computer to do a word search on the word "father." I thought it was strange that I was told to "listen" to it. I am not being dogmatic about this; I really feel I heard the sweet Holy Spirit whisper in my ear.

I pulled up a concordance on a Web site and clicked on the Hebrew word *ab* that is translated "father." From there, I went to the first place it was used in the Old Testament in Genesis 2:24: *Therefore a man shall leave his father and mother and be joined to his wife, and they shall become one flesh.*

After reading the verse, I proceeded to a Web site where I could click on *ab* and hear its pronunciation. I clicked on the word. As it was pronounced, I gasped. The sound was so familiar. As a matter of fact, we all hear it, all the time. Let me explain.

Could I ask you to do something? I would like us to have an interactive moment. Don't worry if you are on a plane or sitting where people are watching you, they will only think you are yawning. Here we go. As you do this, think of someone giving you mouth-to-mouth resuscitation. Open your mouth really wide, as if you are going to yawn. Now take in a very deep, slow, but forceful breath through your mouth. Now, quickly close your mouth and hold it for a second.

Did you hear that sound?
A-w-w-w-b!
Do it again.
A-w-w-w-b!
*Do you hear the **"a-w-w-w"** sound as you are pulling air into your lungs?*
*Do you hear the **"b"** sound as you close you mouth?*

That sound is the Hebrew word for "father." Alphabetically, it is also the first word in the Hebrew Lexicon. *"A-w-w-w-b"* is the sound it makes. Though this may be somewhat speculative, at least the symbolic power of it still gives us a picture of what the Bible tells us about the heart of God toward us. If there is substance to this, then the first human word ever spoken was father. Think of what Father and son felt. Heavenly Father kissed His son with the breath of life, and Adam responded by saying, "Father."

As I studied this I was interested to find that *The Theological Wordbook* denotes that the word "Ab" linguistically actually comes from the primal sound of a baby. Notice the following quotation:

Father, forefather. This primitive noun apparently is derived from such baby sounds as Abab (cf. "Papa," in TDNT, V, p. 960), rather than from the verbal root °bh , Assyrian, Abû "decide" (suggesting that the father is the "decider," BDB, p. 3). It designates primarily "begetter," though by extension, ancestor, and metaphorically, an originator, chief, or associate in some degree.[10]

Isn't it exciting to think that the first word out of Adam's mouth may have very well been the word "Father?" He opened his perfect eyes. What did they see first? They saw his Father's face. His perfect ears opened to hear their first sound and what did they hear? They heard the voice of God. His sense of touch came to life. What sensation did he first feel? He felt the breath of God, the presence of God upon his life. His emotions began functioning, and they were soaked with the love of God. They were bathed in the peace of God. This is what you also were made for, dear friend. The Father's love filled Adam's entire being in that first moment of existence. He still does this for us. The Apostle Paul wrote that the Holy Spirit sheds the love of God abroad in our hearts.

In the introduction, I mentioned that the revelation contained in this book started flowing at a Grandparents' Day that was being hosted at my children's school. As I sat there in the audience, I watched class after class of children take the stage to share their special poem, song, or skit with all the parents and grandparents in attendance. Like most of the adults there, my wife and I were waiting to see our children on the stage. We are the proud parents of four children. On this particular day, our two younger sons, Elliott and Nathan, were to be on stage. Nathan's class finally took the stage. Our eyes were focused on him as his class marched up to the platform to take their places. When Nathan reached his place, he immediately started scanning the audience. We wanted him to see us so badly. We held our hands up hoping to flag his attention. He searched for a minute or so, completely detached from what his class was doing. He was totally disengaged from the song that they had begun singing.

Finally, it happened—his eyes met our eyes. Instantly, a smile swept across his face, and he looked back to the teacher and joined in with his class. Every few seconds, his eyes would dart toward us to make sure we were still watching. When Elliott's turn came to mount the stage with his class, he did the same thing. I began observing the other children and discovered they were doing the same thing. None of them was very concerned about all the other people. They were looking for the face of their parent or grandparent. They just wanted to know if Dad and Mom, or Granddad or Grandma were there. Seeing these children looking for their daddies and mommies unlocked something inside of me. We got this desire from Adam. We were created to look for Father's face. We were made to behold the beauty of the face of God. We cannot be completely satisfied until we do. After the fall, men were not to see the face of God for fear of death. Before the fall, beholding His face was what life was all about. When Jesus died, He restored us so that we too can behold the Father's face.

Think of the pain of wanting Daddy and being unable to find him. On that Grandparents' Day, I thought about all the kids who looked and never saw their father's face because he wasn't there. I thought about those who wouldn't see their father's face when they got home either. I thought of those whose fathers were there but they never found them in the audience. I began to realize that all of us are as Nathan and Elliott were that day. We all want to know that Daddy is watching. We need to know that He is there. It gives us security to be in His presence. We feel so loved to know His eyes are upon us. This feeling, or rather this *need*, is rooted in Adam's experience in the garden. The first face he saw was that of Father God's. We all need the first breath experience so that we are filled with the assurance of Father God's presence in our lives. This is how Jesus lived His life moment by moment.

> *Then Jesus answered and said to them, "Most assuredly, I say to you, the Son can do nothing of Himself, but what He sees the Father do; for whatever He does, the Son also does in like manner."*
>
> John 5:19

> *Then Jesus said to them, "When you lift up the Son of Man, then you will know that I am He, and that I do nothing of Myself; but as My Father taught Me, I speak these things. And He who sent Me is with Me. The Father has not left Me alone, for I always do those things that please Him."*
>
> John 8:28-29

Jesus only did what He saw the Father doing. This means that He lived with His eyes on His Father. He spoke what He heard the Father speak. He lived with His ears tuned to the Father's voice. This is how we are to live. This is how the first Adam lived prior to the fall. This is how Jesus, who is called the last Adam (1 Co 15:45), lived in order to deliver and restore us from the fall of man. I did a word search through the New King James Version Bible and found that "father" in its various forms occurs 1,712 times in the entire Bible. It is used 1,285 times in the Old Testament and 427 times in the New Testament. "Father" is an important word. I believe it was the first word man ever spoke. When the Holy Spirit moves upon the human spirit, the yearning of a child wanting Father's love begins to be fulfilled.

EIGHT

DADDY'S LOVE

There's no pillow quite so soft as a father's strong shoulder.
Richard. L. Evans

While being at my wife's side during all four of our children's deliveries, I gained great respect for what a woman goes through to become a mother. How vividly I can recall the feeling that swept through my soul like a hurricane bringing that *first love*. It is an absolutely amazing love that explodes from parents' hearts the first time they hold the little bundle of life. This is another of those first moment experiences that changes things. Before the baby arrives, you think you know what it's going to be like, but as soon as the baby is born, you realize you didn't have a clue!

Babies are life-changers. On December 9, 1982, our first child, Andrew, was born. Of course, the room was tense with emotion and anticipation as Mikki's contractions grew closer together. Having never had such an experience, I was somewhat nervous as I watched the doctor and nurses do what they were accustomed to doing every day. I found out why they call it *labor*. They certainly named it right.

Finally, when our little boy broke through into the wide-open world in which he would live, he was welcomed with a swat on the rear end. This was the doctor's way of jump-starting Andrew. It's probably not the best way to welcome a little one into the world, but it definitely encourages them to take in that first breath. I wonder if a doctor would just blow in a baby's face, if that might do the job just as well. This is how Father God did it. With Andrew and the swat delivered, our son took his first breath and started crying. Actually, it was more like screaming. The moment Andrew gasped and took in his first breath—we melted. We were so relieved to hear this sound and what a beautiful sound it was! Hearing the first breath of our son turned our anticipation into celebration. The first breath is the sound of life.

Moments later, I was able to hold my son in my arms. I looked into his face marveling at the miracle of life. I was looking at an extension of myself. I was immersed in this indescribable love. I had never felt the particular brand of love that suddenly overtook me. It was an introduction to an affection that had eluded me until that moment, and its intensity caught me off guard. Where did this powerful new emotion come from? Suddenly, onboard equipment that I had never used before started operating within me. I was feeling like a father. This love inside of me toward my child was now motivating me to think in ways I had never thought. It would affect all my future plans. My world had changed. I would now do anything to protect, provide, and care for my son. Mikki felt the same way. He came from us, and he belonged to us. He was born into an atmosphere of love. This desire to provide and protect came from Father God. The Bible teaches us that God is love: *He who does not love does not know God, for God is love* (1 Jo 4:8).

When Adam opened his eyes to experience God, he also experienced love. Love was his first emotion. As a matter of fact, his emotions were activated by love. Until the day that he and his bride, Eve, disobeyed God, he knew no emotion, action, or thought that was contrary to love. Adam was created by love, created in love, created for love, and created to love.

Also, think of the love that was pouring out of Father God's heart the moment He heard Adam's first breath. How His heart must have melted within Him as He witnessed the coming to life of His child! He was able to look into the eyes of someone who was an extension of Himself. For the first time, He was looking into the face of another being made in His image: *So God created man in His own image; in the image of God He created him; male and female He created them* (Ge 1:27).

After the first child is born, some would think the birth of the second would be somewhat diminished in comparison to the first.

This is not so. There may be less nervousness about what is going to happen or the process involved, but the level of excitement in seeing that little one enter the world is the same. Each of the arrivals of our four children was filled with its own miracles and invaded by a new download of love for each of them. The sound of the first breath never diminishes in its wonder. When you were born, Father God rejoiced at the wonder of *you* just as He did Adam.

At my own birth, I was not able to take my first breath. An emergency surgery was performed to deliver me. The umbilical cord had wrapped itself around my neck multiple times, and I was literally choked to death during the process of childbirth. I was pronounced dead and laid aside while they worked feverishly to save my mother's life. After about 15 minutes, when my mother was stabilized, a nurse began working with me and I resuscitated. My parents were told that I would never walk or talk. They were informed that I had extensive brain damage and would be like a vegetable. But God, who gave me breath, had different plans. Praise His name! He has a plan for your life as well. He breathed upon you to become what He ordained you to become. Child of God, He is for you and not against you. Don't underestimate the ability of the Spirit of God to bring about God's perfect plan for your life. God loves you. Just as He had a plan for Adam, He has a plan for you. He wants to fill you with His love and with His Spirit. You were created to live in an atmosphere of love just as Adam was. The God of love welcomed Adam into this world. Adam's entire being reverberated with love. Until you experience the love of God, you will feel unwelcome and unfulfilled in this world.

NINE

WE NEED OUR DADDY!

*There is no fear in love; but perfect love casts out fear,
because fear involves torment. But he who fears
has not been made perfect in love.*

1 John 4:18

Several years ago, I was involved in counseling a couple whose
marriage had been deeply threatened by the wife's infidelity. I
vividly remember the husband describing the heart-wrenching
pain that he went through. This Christian man shared how he
struggled to find an answer to what he should do. He had enjoyed
a close relationship with his father, but his father had died a few
years earlier. He had always been able to talk to his dad and draw
from his fatherly wisdom. Seeking answers, he went for a drive in
the middle of a rainy night and ended up at his father's grave. He
shared with me that he laid on his father's grave in the rain and
wept. He needed his daddy! This was as close as he could get to his
dad in the circumstances. Fortunately, he found grace from his
Heavenly Father, and the marriage was spared. It was even made
stronger through the power of forgiveness and the grace of God. Father God promises to be a father to the fatherless. He is Daddy God
to His children!

I am aware there will be those who will accuse me of being irrev-
erent in referring to the awesome God of this universe in such an in-
formal way. I cannot help it; He's my Daddy God! There will be

those who think that I have hurdled mindlessly over the foundational doctrine of holiness. Others will find themselves struggling with revulsion at the notion that the supreme God of all creation could be spoken of in such earthly tones. I cannot help it; He's my Daddy God. This is not an attempt to undo the great doctrinal truths concerning the attributes of the great God of the universe. It is about intimacy. It is about the discovery that every son and daughter must make if they are to experience the true fatherhood of God. There is no denying that He is Father. Jesus called Him such and taught us to pray, *Our Father in heaven, Hallowed be Your name* (Ma 6:9). The intellectual understanding of God as Father, and the spiritual intimacy that Father makes available to us, can be worlds apart. If you are a believer in Jesus—you can call Him "Daddy God" without fear of reproach.

The term *Abba Father* is used in the New Testament to describe the believer's relationship to God. The *Exegetical Dictionary of the New Testament* contains the following explanation of the word *abba*: "Abba in Aramaic was originally a nursery word, part of the speech of children (not the determinative form of the noun 'father'), with the meaning 'Daddy.'" The phrase is a term of endearment. It expresses fondness and affection from the heart of the child to his or her father. There are three occasions when *abba* is employed in the New Testament.

The first occasion is when Jesus, in intense agony, prayed in Gethsemane's garden. The weight of the cross and the world's sins were looming before Him. He was spending time with His Heavenly Father. As He prays, He cries out to God as *Abba, Father*. He was about to step into the biggest storm of His life, and He needed His Daddy! Read what Mark, the Gospel writer, records: *And He said, "Abba, Father, all things are possible for You. Take this cup away from Me; nevertheless, not what I will, but what You will"* (Mk 14:36).

Jesus prayed knowing that if anyone could help Him, it would be His Daddy. All things are possible for Daddy. Isn't this how we felt as little kids? In our times of crisis, we need Daddy. Just recently, I received a phone call from my daughter, Kara Beth. "Daddy," she said, "I just had a wreck." Of course, it staggered me a little bit. I asked her if she was all right. To my relief, she and the people in the other car were all uninjured. The damage was minor. I reassured her that everything was fine and that I was so thankful she was not hurt. I told her cars could be fixed. The point is this—when trouble came, she needed her daddy. She wanted to talk to her daddy. We all like a daddy who is strong and can take care of us.

The second occurrence of the word *abba* is found in Romans 8:15: *For you did not receive the spirit of bondage again to fear, but you received the Spirit of adoption by whom we cry out, "Abba, Father."* The Apostle Paul uses the expression *Abba, Father* after sharing the truth that we have been adopted into God's family as His children. This means we can relate to Him as Daddy, our Father. He is not to be seen as an aloof and remote deity who is out there somewhere. He is a loving Father who is here with us in the here and now. We do not have to be afraid of Him as though He were angry with us. He wants a Father-child relationship with us that is motivated by love instead of fear.

When our middle son, Elliott, was two years old, we attended a Christmas parade. He was Mommy's boy. He would play with me, but he didn't want to get too far away from his mommy's arms. However, as the Christmas parade made its way through the city streets, the fire engines sounded their sirens. As they drove near us, it became very loud. Elliott, who was safe in his mother's arms, began to cry for me. He was frightened, and he wanted Daddy to protect him. Children run to Mother to be nurtured, but they run to *Daddy* to be protected.

There is something wrong in an earthly home where children are continually afraid to approach their father. I have been amazed in these past few years at the number of people, especially women, I have ministered to who have been subjected to terrible types of abuse by their fathers, step-fathers, or other male authority figures in their lives. The enemy has a hey-day in the house where such mistreatment takes place. Think of it, a little girl or boy grows up in a house with Mom and Dad. This house represents the physical location where love, security, acceptance, provision, and discipline are to take place. All these combine to help shape this little child's attitudes and beliefs about life. There can be some failure in good homes where intentions and desires are strongly set in the direction of godliness. However, there are other homes where little or no thought is given about what is taking place in the souls of the little children.

In addition, other parents who strongly desire their children to be shaped correctly use the wrong tools to do the shaping. They employ harshness, coarseness, anger, and rejection. These tools are ignorantly used to attempt to build a structure of godliness. Yet, it is clear from Scripture that these tools are not available in the Holy Spirit's supply room. How odd that we could be deceived into using the devil's tools to attempt to build God's house. A child can be taught to avoid doing wrong in a variety of ways. But the same child also can feel alone, unloved, rejected, and hopeless. That same child can be made to be obedient in a machine-like manner but void of the fulfillment that closeness, intimacy, and security bring. That child also will have difficulty with intimacy in all their relationships. A man can be a wonderful provider of those things that bring "material" security into the lives of his wife and children and be clueless to the needs they have for true intimacy. We do not have to be afraid. We are not in bondage anymore to fear. We are adopted into Daddy God's family.

The third occasion when *Abba, Father* is used is in Galatians 4:6: *And because you are sons, God has sent forth the Spirit of His Son into your hearts, crying out, "Abba, Father!"* Notice Paul writes that God has sent the Spirit of His Son into our hearts. Wow! Just as Jesus related to Father, so can we. We are sons and daughters of God. The Holy Spirit inside of us cries out to God as *Abba.* He truly is Daddy God to us. The reality that we are sons and daughters of God is a truth, when properly understood, releases great blessing into the hearts of God's children.

It seems as a teenager, I was always destined to be caught in my sin. If I tried something, most of the time I was caught—the first time! After I graduated high school, I went to college. I lived on campus, which ended up giving me a lot of idle time. I would go to my room from my daily classes, study, do homework, and then look for ways to spend my time until bedtime. In our boredom, a friend and I found ourselves playing *daredevil*. We would dare one another to do certain things to see if we could get away with it. It really added some exhilaration to our rather mundane lives, but it only lasted about two days. That's how long it was before we were busted. I was so humiliated. I felt that my stupidity had cost me all my dreams. A deep depression swept over me. I felt so utterly hopeless. My parents had been so proud of me. Now, I had disgraced my whole family.

I went through the embarrassment of dealing with the police, and finally we were released. My friend and I were charged with malicious mischief. Since I was away from home at college, I thought I could hide the incident from Dad and Mom. The next day I was preparing to go home, and my sister called me. "Ed," she said, "they know." How could they know? How did my sister know? What would I do now? Be sure your sins will find you out. Boy, was I in trouble!

My dad and mom had always loved me, but I dreaded the trip home that night. I deserved whatever they chose to do to me. I was so low, I could have played handball against the curb. I drove up into our driveway, parked the car, walked through the door into the kitchen, and started the dreaded trip down the hallway to the room where my dad was waiting. With my head hanging, I walked into Dad and Mom's bedroom. I braced for what was coming. Daddy looked at me and said, "Son, we all make mistakes. Everything is going to be all right. I love you."

I ran into his arms and began sobbing. At that moment, I was eight instead of 18. I needed my daddy, and he was there for me. He would have been justified in giving me the fifth degree. He could have verbally chewed me up one side and down the other telling me how I had blown it. He could have told me what I did went against everything he had ever taught me. Instead, he loved me. I have never forgotten what my daddy did that night. It was one of the darkest nights of my life, and he loved me. His arms and his love embraced me in the middle of my failure. Just as Father God went to Adam and Eve in love and provided a covering for them in the middle of their failure, my dad covered me with his love.

This is what Father God did for us through the cross. He so loved us that He gave His only Son. The blood of Jesus covers us in our failures and enables us to feel the loving embrace of the arms of Daddy God. Our sin makes us want to hide. His love brings us into the light where we can be cleansed by the blood of Jesus. Our sin will drive us from those who love us the most. It did so in the garden, and it has the same effect on people today. Even in the shame and stain of our sin, Father desires to reach out to rescue us. His redemptive love is tenacious and strong.

Now, don't get me wrong, there is a place for discipline. My dad disciplined me for my daredevil antics, but first he loved me. Discipline is bearable when it is delivered in the arms of love. The Bible teaches us that whom the Father loves, He disciplines. There is a difference in discipline that is administered by an angry man and discipline that is administered by a loving father. I never doubted that my dad and mom loved me. Not once have I ever questioned their love for me. I know that many people cannot make such a statement, but I am grateful that I can. Love is such a powerful force. The Bible says, "Love never fails."

Years later, after I had graduated from seminary, I was visiting with my Dad. He had been diagnosed with leukemia. He and I walked out to his workshop where he was showing me some of his new tools. Dad was a carpenter by trade and taught me the trade as well. He and I had built several houses together and at one time had a cabinet shop together. We enjoyed talking about his workshop and tools for a while. As we prepared to walk back to the mobile home in which he was living, I stopped him.

"Dad," I said. "I need to talk to you a minute."

"Sure," he said.

"Dad, I just want to tell you that I have never doubted that you love me. I want you to know how much that means to me. Even during the times I wasn't so easy to love, you still loved me. You will never know how much it has meant to me to have a Daddy that believed in me and loved me."

I could tell that the words meant a lot to my dad. Of course, he responded by loving me. We hugged and went back to his house. Not many months later, unexpectedly, Daddy went home to be with Jesus. I miss him. I was attending a conference in New Orleans, Louisiana, when Daddy died. He slipped away in his sleep in the middle of the night. At 4:00 a.m., I awakened and sat up in bed. I knew something strange was going on. My daddy was heavy on my heart. In a few minutes, the telephone rang. My wife called to tell me that Dad had just died. I hung up and got on my knees at the foot of the bed. I thanked God for my daddy and I talked to him, just as if he were there with me. I expressed my love and my regrets to him. At that moment, I was hit with the truth that there was so much more I should have done for Dad than I had done. There was so much more that I could have said that I did not say. I agonized over the fact that Daddy had done so much more for me than I had ever done for him. I prayed, thanking my Heavenly Father for giving me my earthly father. I miss my daddy. I look forward to seeing him again when Daddy God gathers all His kids together. He has planned an awesome reunion for us all.

Just a few weeks ago, I attended a conference titled *Embracing the Father's Love*. It was led by a man by the name of Jack Frost. The teaching was very powerful, and so many lives were touched by the Father's love. At the conclusion of the first night's service, people all over the building were weeping. Jack had shared how he and his father were reconciled after years of having a stormy relationship. It was obvious that many people in attendance had painful issues in regard to their fathers. As I witnessed the brokenness and sobbing all around me, I was overcome by this deep sense of gratitude. I realized the pain I had been spared in my life because of the way my dad and mom loved me. I sat there and thought, "How many successes have I enjoyed in life because I knew my daddy loved me? How many difficulties have I been spared because I did not struggle with feeling unloved?" I have had to deal with rejection issues in my life, but not because I felt unloved at home. We all need a daddy to love us.

My daddy used to utterly embarrass me by bragging on me. To him, I was just the greatest son a man could have. I remember an occasion at the first church I ever pastored when my dad made his first visit. He made the two-hour drive one Sunday morning to hear his boy preach. I had not preached very many times, and I was what we call in the South "gourd-green." At the conclusion of the service, my dad asked if he could say something. What could I say? He was my daddy. Dad walked up to the platform and behind the pulpit. He then addressed the congregation, "I know you have not known Eddie very long. Let me tell you how blessed you are to have him as your pastor." It got worse from that point. I was so embarrassed. My face turned red. I was thinking, "Daddy, don't do this!" He believed in me and loved me so much. He was going to make sure that everyone in the church knew how special his son was. I would love to hear him now. I would gladly listen to anything he wanted to say.

I have grown to appreciate the truth that I have a Daddy God! I can sit in His lap, so to speak, and feel the warmth of His embrace, and know that I am shielded from all the bad things that are happening around me. He is Daddy God to me. He is Daddy God to you as well. We need our Daddy!

We were made to be loved by Father because we were made by the love of Father. One of the wicked works of the devil involves destroying relationships between fathers and their children. Before the Second Coming of Jesus Christ, the Spirit of God will be working to return the hearts of the fathers to the children and the children to the fathers. God will breathe His breath on fathers and mothers and sons and daughters to turn their hearts toward Him and each other.

As you continue to read, you will see how Father God intended His first human son and daughter to relate. Adam and Eve were literally made for each other. Let's look at the first marriage!

TEN

THE FIRST MARRIAGE

Keep your eyes wide open before marriage, and half shut afterwards.
Benjamin Franklin

*So Adam gave names to all cattle, to the birds of the air, and to every
beast of the field. But for Adam there was not found a helper
comparable to him.*
Genesis 2:20

A question that I have been pondering in recent days is, "Why
did God allow Adam to look through all the animal kingdom
for a helpmate?" He knew Adam would not find his helpmate
among the lower beings. Why did He want Adam to experience this
process?

I have concluded it was so Adam would know there was nothing
else in God's creation that could complete his human needs. The
destiny that God had ordained for man could only be completed
with someone else bearing the image of God.

God took a rib from Adam's side to bring forth a woman to be
his bride. God made a perfect bride to give to His perfect son. This
was the perfect marriage with a perfect beginning in a perfect place.
In their sinless state, Adam and Eve enjoyed the most intimate, loving relationship that has ever existed between a husband and wife.
Their relationship before their fall into sin is a picture of the rela-

tionship that Christ desires to have with His bride, the church. In the New Testament letter to the Ephesians, the Apostle Paul teaches us that marriage is a picture of the relationship between Christ and the church. *For we are members of His body, of His flesh and of His bones.* *"For this reason a man shall leave his father and mother and be joined to his wife, and the two shall become one flesh." This is a great mystery, but I speak concerning Christ and the church* (Ep 5:30-32).

God later placed His seed inside the womb of the virgin Mary and brought forth another man, Jesus. Jesus was the promised deliverer, the Messiah. He came to reverse the curse brought on by the sin of Adam. When Jesus came, it marked the beginning of the restoration of all things that man had lost through his fall into sin. Adam gave of himself to produce Eve. Jesus gave all of Himself to produce His bride.

In marriage, the laws of mathematics work differently. In marriage 1 + 1 = 1, and when a child arrives, 1 + 1 = 3. This is because a husband and wife become one flesh. They are no longer to view themselves independently of one another. Marriage is an exclusive covenant. When you marry, you become unavailable in many ways to any other person on the planet. Do not view this as restrictive, for it is not. Actually, it brings completion. Don't be like the foolish man who said, "Marriage made me complete. When I got married, it finished me off." Adam was created in perfection, but yet he was not complete because God said, *It is not good that man should be alone* (Ge 2:18). God took a rib out of Adam's side and created Eve. Then God brought her to Adam.

The fact that Eve was brought by God to Adam means that before she met Adam she had already met God. Eve's first encounter was with God. The first face the first woman ever saw was the face of God. The first voice she ever heard was the voice of God. The first conscious awareness she ever experienced was of the presence of God. She, like Adam, awakened into an incredible atmosphere of love. Her Heavenly Father then walked her down the aisle of the Garden of Eden and gave her to her bridegroom, Adam.

She came from Adam by creation, but she was given to Adam by choice. God made Eve for Adam, but before she was ready for Adam, she first had to meet God. This is the pattern for Christian marriage today. God brings a woman who has met Him into the life of a man who has met Him, and then they meet each other and become one. They are then truly able to view the other as a gift from God.

God brought forth Eve out of Adam's side. Similarly, God birthed the church, which is called the bride of Christ, out of the side of His Son, Jesus. This is the act of the new creation. Though the church came from the Son, before the church can be given to the Son, she must first have an experience with God the Father. Every believer goes to the Father through the Son (Jo 14:6).

Eve came into the presence of God out of the side of her husband, Adam. She came to the Father through His perfect son, Adam. Adam was put to sleep, and a rib was taken out of his side. God made Eve. As someone aptly said, she was a "GM" model. She was God-made. God's creative work made her perfect and suitable for her husband. After this creative work of God in which Eve was given life, He then presented her back to Adam and ordained that they become one.

The first marriage was one in which the husband and wife enjoyed a wonderful, uninterrupted flow of communication. There were no arguments or misunderstandings. This is what Jesus also desires with His bride, the church. The bride of Christ must realize that she is passionately loved by her bridegroom. He bends His ear toward her, hearing the words of love she whispers toward Him. She also must learn to hear His voice calling to her. There will always be other voices trying to woo the affections of her heart away from her bridegroom. When she refuses these voices, there is an intensification of her love toward Jesus. When she fails to resist these voices, the consequences can be disastrous.

The day that Eve listened to the serpent, things changed for all humanity. When she gave the fruit to her husband, Adam, and he ate with her, the communication between husband and wife became marred. Ever since that time, the voice of woman has suffered. However, when Jesus died on the cross, He broke the power of the curse. He did more to bring value and honor back to women than any man who has ever lived. By His self-abandonment, He lifted women from the degraded status of slaves to that of redeemed brides worthy of sacrificial love. Adam and Eve walked, talked, and ruled together. Jesus and His bride now walk, talk, and rule together in the realm of Earth. Before the fall, Adam and Eve had a mutual respect and honor for each other that had not been corrupted by sin. Eve, as Adam's perfect bride, was a picture of the church who will be Christ's perfect bride.

Marriage is a picture of Christ and His church. Husbands, you need to realize that Christ listens to His bride. He lives to make intercession for her. He does not ignore her. He gives Himself to her. There are times when Father wants to speak to us through our wives, but we resist because of the occasion when the serpent spoke to Adam through his wife. Deep in our DNA, this is an attitude that we carry toward women. We are quick to assume that their counsel is not worthy of our respect.

I am reminded of an incident that happened a few years ago in which God used my wife to speak to me. This occurred on a Wednesday night at the conclusion of a service in which I had just preached. We had eaten a meal together, and it was followed by a worship service in the fellowship hall. At the conclusion of the service, one of the sweet little ladies of the church approached me. She said, "Brother Eddie, that message was so wonderful. The whole time that you were preaching, I saw a halo over your head." She went on and on about seeing the halo. In a few moments, she had me feeling like quite the angel. I thought, "Yea, a halo! Wow! Was I anointed or what?"

I strutted home to the parsonage where we lived at the time. I entered the house waltzing in glory thinking about how the Lord had given visual evidence of my preaching prowess. What an anointing must have fallen upon me. It must have been reminiscent of the transfiguration of Jesus. Mikki, who had arrived home earlier, walked down the hall toward me. I was preparing to tell her about this great manifestation of glory that had fallen upon me while I had been preaching. I thought she might not have noticed it. Before I could address her, she stopped, and blurted out, "You need to get someone to adjust the spotlights in the fellowship hall. The whole time you were preaching tonight, they were glaring off your bald head." Oh! What a dagger to the heart! I tried to accuse her of not being nearly as spiritual as the little lady at the church. As I said, sometimes the Lord speaks to husbands through their wives. They often carry the punch that needs to be delivered to our pride to keep us humble. Seriously, how much pain could a husband avoid if he paid as much attention to his bride as Jesus does His? Aren't you glad that Jesus listens to His bride? The enemy is still actively working to keep husbands from honoring their wives and to keep wives from honoring their husbands. He is also working to shut down communication between Christ and His bride. Pilate's wife came to him as he was deciding the fate of Jesus. She shared that she had a dream the night before about the matter. She warned Pilate to have nothing to do with the matter. He ignored her and look at the pain that was caused to Christ's body (Ma 27:19). There is a lesson here for us husbands. Often, we bring pain upon the body of Christ because our fallen nature resists the counsel of our wives. We must realize that the daughters of Eve have been redeemed just as we have.

At the cross, most of the sons of Adam ran, but the daughters of Eve remained. They were able to witness the fulfillment of the Word that Father God had prophesied over the serpent. They saw God's promised seed crushing the serpent's head. They may not have been aware of it at that moment, but their destiny as women was being redeemed. Three days later, Father would allow one of Eve's daughters to be the first to proclaim the resurrection. As usual, the men refused to listen to the women. They went to check it out for themselves and discovered that the woman's voice had faithfully delivered the good news to them (Lk 24:11). Men must learn to respect and receive from their wives. Otherwise, the marriage will not be what God intends for it to be. Often, their sensitivity to the Spirit of God will give them discernment that we men are lacking. On the day of Pentecost, when Father breathed on the church, men and women were gathered together in unity awaiting Father's promise.

Adam and Eve, the perfect son and his perfect wife, ultimately failed Father. God had a plan to redeem His fallen children. Jesus, the last Adam, came and laid down His life in the sleep of death so that His Father could take from His side what was needed to make a wife suitable for Him. The bride of Christ comes to the Father through the Son. When this happens, God begins the work of making her all she needs to be in order to present her back to His Son. There will come a day when she will be presented to Jesus, and she will have no spots, blemishes, wrinkles, or any such thing (Ep 5:27). She came from His side, and she will stand as bride at His side. God has ordained that we, as the bride of Christ, are to be one with Him.

At the cross, perfect purity was met by complete corruption. The judgment of death was given, but the power of sin was broken. This is the only time that sin ever did or ever will cause a pause in the sweet communion that has eternally existed within the Trinity. Theologians call this the "great exchange." The sinless Son of God became sin, so that sinful men could become sons of God. *For He made Him who knew no sin to be sin for us, that we might become the righteousness of God in Him* (2 Co 5:21).

Father God commanded Adam and Eve to be fruitful, multiply, and fill the earth. Here again we see a glimpse of God's purposes. He wanted the earth to be filled with sons and daughters who would bear His image, who would live in His presence, who would see His face, who would hear His voice, and who would live by His river. This is the heart of God for you as well. This is what is meant by marriages made in heaven. A person once asked Mother Teresa, "What can I do to promote world peace?" She responded, "Go home and love your family!" In reality, if we cannot be a Christian in our home, we cannot be a true Christian anywhere. Is the fragrance of heaven filling your home? Is your marriage a reflection of the relationship between Christ and His bride?

Another thought to consider concerning the beautiful oneness that existed between Adam and Eve prior to the fall has to do with their agreement. In their communion and their communication, they were always in agreement. Before they sinned, they never operated contrary to God's desires. Their wills were always in agreement with each other and with God. This is a beautiful picture of what happens when believers pray in agreement with the desires of God. I personally believe that one of the most powerful prayers that can be prayed is that of a Christian husband and wife praying a prayer of agreement. In marriage, the two become one. In Christian marriage, the man and woman should be one in spirit, soul, and body. When this prayer of agreement is released in agreement with what God wants to do, powerful results follow. There is no doubt that Adam and Eve had a perfect marriage. In the next chapter, we will discuss some of the great benefits of their early days together. They had it all before the fall.

ELEVEN

THE "NEVERS" AND "ALWAYS'" OF ADAM'S LIFE

꒰ ⤳

All I have seen teaches me to trust the Creator for all I have not seen.
Ralph Waldo Emerson

The blessings of Adam and Eve's unity before the fall are exciting. Think of the things that Adam never experienced until he
experienced sin. He never knew what it was to have his conscience
attack him. He never had an argument with his wife. He never ran
a fever. He never had a stomachache. He never spent a day sick in
bed. He never lost his temper. He never cursed. He never doubted
God. He never faced a fear. He never had to confess his sin to God.
He never had to offer a sacrifice. He never was scratched by a brier.
He never experienced any kind of lack concerning anything he
needed. He never attended a funeral. He never saw anything die.
He never shed a tear in sorrow. He never experienced evil of any
kind. He never mistreated anyone nor was he ever mistreated by
anyone. He never was convicted for a sin he committed because he
never committed a sin. Lust never conquered him. He was never
unfaithful to his wife. He was truly a one-woman man. Covetous-
ness never found a place in him. He did not struggle against a fallen

nature. He never battled hate. He never experienced rejection. He never harbored bitterness in his heart. He never failed at anything he did. He never knew the agony of defeat. He never procrastinated nor became too busy. He never struggled in his walk with God. These were some of the "nevers" that were part of Adam's life before sin entered Adam's life.

Likewise, the "always'" of Adam's life before he sinned are very revealing. Adam always sensed the presence of God in his life. Adam always obeyed God. Adam always felt loved and accepted by his wife and God. Adam always heard God speak when He spoke to him. Adam always had his requests heard and answered by God. Adam always slept well. Adam always had joy in his heart. Adam always had peace in his heart. Adam always was right when he shared something with his wife. Adam always enjoyed good health. Adam always had the wisdom and power to do what was right. Adam always properly exercised dominion in the earth. Adam always experienced productivity in his work. Adam always saw the good in all of God's creation. Adam always had pure thoughts. Adam always loved his wife with a pure heart. Adam always saw what his Father was doing and did it. Adam was always kind. Adam always walked in the Spirit. Adam always was filled with the Spirit. Adam was always perfect. Adam always walked in love. Adam always lived in faith that always pleased God. Of course all of this was equally true for his wife, Eve.

These "always" and "nevers" help us to see God's intentions for the first man and the first woman. They also help us to understand the major shift that occurred in the earth when man sinned. Understanding what was originally man's that has been forfeited due to sin helps us to yearn for the restoration of man's privileged position before Father God. This restoration was set in motion by the Lord Jesus Christ when He died and arose from the dead. He continues to move in restoration power changing things through His Spirit working in His church on the earth.

An encouraging thought in the midst of the sorrow brought on by the curse of sin is this: though sin has changed man's heart toward God, it did not change God's heart toward man. God is intent on manifesting His love in the human heart and seeing this thing come out right. He is God and He has the power and capacity to see His desires accomplished. Now, some may say, how can God rightly do this? They say God had a plan in the beginning and it went South on Him. Dear reader, you do not understand. God is not busy trying to figure out what His next move is going to be. God doesn't even have a next move. Move implies sequence and reaction. God does not react. God knows all and has always known all. He has never been caught off guard, nor will He ever be. He does not plan as He goes because He does not go—He simply is. He abides in the now of eternity, unbound and unlimited by time as we know it. Adam and Eve did not spring a surprise on God. God has never been surprised. Yet, He is the God of surprises. He always ends up on top of every situation and circumstance. He does not call an emergency meeting in the courts of heaven where our fates are decided as the options are explored. No! He simply rules as God knowing all! You can't check-mate God. God always has a play that will turn things around. He has never had to experience adrenalin rush. Don't make the mistake of thinking He has a rather boring existence. He enjoys watching how we respond and work through our situations even though He knows what we are going to do. Like watching a 2-year-old head for the candy on the coffee table, the parent knows what he is going to do once he gets there, but he still enjoys watching the process. When you know every thought a person thinks, then you are never caught off-guard by their actions. God knows our thoughts. More than that, He knows our thoughts before we ever think them. Whoa! How can such a thing be? It is part and parcel of being God! Everything that exists in the universe has been engineered and designed by Him. It is held together by the word of His power.

A compass always points to magnetic North unless there is some type of electromagnetic interference. When there is interference, the person following the compass will end up missing the mark of their destination. Likewise, man was made so that his point of reference would always be God. Knowing and being with God is the originally intended grand goal of humanity. When there is interference, he misses the mark. Deep in your DNA there is a pull toward God. The interference of sin, the devil, and our fallen nature cause us to think we are moving toward life's grand goal when we are really missing the mark. Some would dare suggest that all roads of religion lead to God. This is as absurd as thinking that heading east will take you north. You must have the right reference point without interference to stay on track.

Jesus, our great intercessor, prayed for us to all become one the night before He was crucified. The power of unity in marriage and in the church is much greater than we can imagine. This is one of the reasons the enemy works so hard to divide and conquer. The devil, the great accuser, is always releasing his voice to drive us apart. As you read on, you shall see how this division always causes pain and sorrow.

SECTION THREE

FATHER'S HEART FOR YOU

Twelve

The Separation

I have been all things unholy.
If God can work through me,
he can work through anyone.

Saint Francis of Assisi

One of the tougher things that Mikki and I have ever been called upon to do was to tell our children that their Papa, Mikki's dad, had died. They loved their Papa and the thought of his absence in their lives was extremely painful. A few years later we had the dreaded task of informing our nephew and niece that their daddy, Mikki's twin brother, had died in a car accident on the way home from work. We had to awaken them out of their sleep to deliver the heartbreaking news to them. Life is filled with its losses and the pain caused by separation. All of us in one way or another have felt the emotional quakes of separation in our lives. Before the fall of man into sin, the only separation was one brought on by blessing—a man would leave his father and mother and be joined to his wife. This resulted in the addition of relationship instead of the subtraction of relationship. After the fall, however, sin unleashed a force into the earth that caused separation on several painful levels.

Sin was the one thing that would bring separation between Father God and His son, Adam. Sin was the one thing that would ruin Eden. Eden's enjoyment would be suspended the moment that sin entered the human race. Sin would sow the seed for death to come and life to end. How grieved God's heart must have been to have seen His son and daughter choosing to disobey Him and forfeit the wonderful fellowship they had all enjoyed.

His heart was broken, but it was also moved with fiery love to redeem what had been lost. It may be that you have a child who has chosen to step away from you. The distance created by their steps has broken your heart. Father God knows how you feel. He was the perfect parent, yet His two perfect kids chose to become imperfect. Oh, how I hate what sin does to us all! It makes a mess of things, doesn't it? It hurts terribly to be separated from the ones you most love. The stinging pain of rejection is potent in its ability to immobilize us. Many succumb to depression because of such situations. We must learn to respond as Father God did. He responded with redemption in His heart. He dared to go after what had been lost. We see Him in Eden's garden pursuing His runaway son and clothing him with skins from an animal that gave its life to provide a covering for sinful man.

We see Him in Gethsemane's garden and on Golgotha's hill allowing Jesus to shed His blood to provide a covering for sinful man. The cross is the greatest proof of the greatest love that man could ever know. Through the cross, the love of God pursued sinful humanity to the death. God chose the place called Golgotha to become the world's garbage dump on the Friday Jesus died. All of our trash, vileness, corruptness, wickedness, and sin were dumped onto the body of Jesus. He bore our sin in His own body on the tree. He was the perfect, giving His life for the imperfect. He was the pure, giving His life for the impure. Why? He did it to bring us back to God. We no longer have to run and hide from our sin as Adam and Eve did. Jesus died openly and publicly, bearing our sins. When we trust in what He did for us, we are enabled once again to live in the open in the presence of God.

Man was not created to serve God from a distance. He was created to experience God face to face. Sin isolates us from God, yet we were created to live in intimacy with God. *But your iniquities have separated you from your God; and your sins have hidden His face from you, so that He will not hear* (Is 59:2). When Adam and Eve sinned against God and chose to obey another rather than Him, they immediately began hiding from God and blaming each other. They experienced shame and separation for the first time in their lives.

They were deceived, and it altered their destiny. This is always the pattern of sin—it eats away at our relationships, beginning with those that are the most important.

Everything that God created for good, Satan desires to distort toward evil. Man and woman were created to be fruitful and multiply. What does Satan do? He enters the garden and begins separating the woman from the man through demonic dialogue. Later, God declares to the serpent that He would bring an offspring through the woman to destroy him. Ever since then, the enemy has sought to destroy woman's offspring. Even in our culture, the enemy is working through abortion to destroy the next generation. Through this, the enemy once again heaps shame and guilt on men and women. God's heart is to forgive, redeem, and restore. His passionate love pursues us to deliver us from the curse of death in all its forms. God is raising up a new generation to usher in spiritual revolution and restore the original intentions of God.

Man and woman were given dominion over the created order. Sin has perverted this, and now man seeks dominion over his brothers and sisters. Man wars against man, and peace flees from the earth.

Human sexuality is a gift from God, and the enemy seeks to distort it by tempting people to violate God's boundary of marriage. Incest, extramarital sex, premarital sex, homosexuality, pornography, pedophilia, and prostitution are all distortions of a beautiful gift given by God to Adam and Eve. What was given to cause multiplication now often causes division.

Sin, in its essence, is breaking God's boundary of love. Loving God and loving others sums up the motivations that should fuel the actions of a man's life. When we place our interests or ambitions ahead of loving God or others, we sin. Adam and Eve chose to go against the Father who loved them, and as a result, love turned into lust; lust turned into sin; sin turned into death.

When the boundary of love was broken by Adam and Eve, sin, lurking at its borders, came rushing in, contaminating everything in its path. This set in motion the law of sin and death. A person's life would now have a terminal point called death. Death is the last breath. Before sin entered the human race, men and women were destined to live forever carrying out the purposes of God in the earth. Many scriptures bear this out. Look at these interesting verses about the last breath.

Abraham, Isaac, and Jacob

> *Then Abraham breathed his last and died in a good old age…*(Ge 25:8).
> *So Isaac breathed his last and died…* (Ge 35:29).
> *And when Jacob had finished commanding his sons, he drew his feet up into the bed and breathed his last, and was gathered to his people* (Ge 49:33).

Ananias and Sapphira Die

> *Then Ananias, hearing these words, fell down and breathed his last* (Ac 5:5).
> *Then immediately she fell down at his feet and breathed her last* (Ac 5:10).

In the New Testament book of James, we are given the biblical definition for bodily death. *For as the body without the spirit is dead* (Ja 2:26). However, just because your body dies doesn't mean that the real "you" dies. The assurance for the believer in Jesus is that our spirit leaves the body to go be with the Lord. *So we are always confident, knowing that while we are at home in the body we are absent from the Lord. For we walk by faith, not by sight. We are confident, yes, well pleased rather to be absent from the body and to be present with the Lord* (2 Co 5:6-8).

I have witnessed the physical death of a number of people during the course of my ministry. One that really stands out in my memory is Sam Brown. Brother Sam was the chairman of deacons in the first church I ever pastored. He also was the church treasurer. He and his wife Ruby were such an encouragement to Mikki and me. Sam was diagnosed with cancer and within three weeks he went to be with the Lord. Emblazoned in my mind is the memory of Brother Sam reaching his hands toward heaven as if seeing someone we could not see. He cried out, "Lord Jesus, come and get me." It wasn't long until he breathed his last breath. At that moment, he was transported into the Lord's literal presence. When we understand the truth, we realize that God gives us our first breath and wants to receive us at our last breath.

Adam was made alive by the first breath. Once the last breath is taken, the body dies. Therefore, the spirit leaves the body through the last breath. This is also seen through the last breath of the last Adam, Jesus. You can release your last breath with confidence when you understand and embrace the message of the cross. Read on and you will discover something about the cross you may have never thought of before.

THIRTEEN

THE LAST BREATH OF THE LAST ADAM

᷑◦᷑

There is no mystery in heaven or earth so great as this—
a suffering Deity, an almighty Saviour nailed to a Cross.
Samuel M. Zwemer

And so it is written, "The first man Adam became a living being." The
last Adam became a life-giving spirit.
1 Corinthians 15:45

Jesus lived by doing what He saw His Father doing and saying what He heard His Father saying. He lived with a conscious awareness that His Father was always with Him. Adam lived with this same awareness until he committed sin and received the awareness of evil into his life. Father God wants us to live with the awareness of His presence.

Jesus came to restore what Adam had lost through sin. Although Adam, his wife Eve, and humanity were made to live forever, their destiny was cut short by sin. Adam's sin unleashed death on us all. We inherited a fallen sin nature from Adam, and we die. Adam's sin caused death to reign on the earth. Jesus came as the last Adam to break the power of death and take away its sting. His resurrection is proof of His victory over death. The first Adam became a death-giver. The last Adam, Jesus, is a life-giver. The last Adam became a life-giving spirit.

When Adam breathed his first breath, he was given life. Later, through disobedience, he became a sinner. His disobedience sealed the day that he would have a last breath experience—death. However, Jesus did something absolutely awesome. He defeated death at its own game!

> *And Jesus said to him, "Assuredly, I say to you, today you will be with Me in Paradise." Now it was about the sixth hour, and there was darkness over all the earth until the ninth hour. Then the sun was darkened, and the veil of the temple was torn in two. And when Jesus had cried out with a loud voice, He said, "Father, 'into Your hands I commit My spirit.'" Having said this, He breathed His last.*
>
> Luke 23:43-46

When Adam breathed his first breath, he awakened in the presence of the Father. When Jesus, the last Adam, breathed His last breath, He was still in submission to the Father. He committed His spirit to His Father. It is important to understand that Jesus became sin; He did not commit sin. Jesus bore our sin; He did not personally engage in sin. He did not commit sin, but He did agree with the Father that man's sin could be committed to Him. His choice to commit personal sin would have placed Him beside the first Adam under the dominion of death. Instead, Jesus, in perfect righteousness, chose to take Adam's place in judgment. He took the wrath of Adam's sin and our sin upon Himself. He did not know sin personally, but chose to bear our sin sacrificially.

In simple terms, we committed the crime, but He stood in our place to be sentenced, condemned, and executed. He was not like a person innocently charged of a crime spending time on death row trying to get an appeal because He had been falsely charged. He is like the person on death row who chose to be there in the place of the person He knew was guilty. He never opens His mouth about it. He goes to the death for another. That "other" was you and I.

Darwinian evolutionists speculate that a species is propagated by the survival of the fittest. They teach their students that only the best in the line survives. Isn't it interesting that God, whom they say does not exist, chose to allow the best of the "species" to die in order that the weaker ones could live? God's ways are truly unsearchable and higher than our ways.

The Bible is clear that Jesus did bear our sins in His own body. This was a sight His Father could not bear; He had to look away. He could have rescued His Son Jesus from the cross, but He turned away from Jesus so that He could turn to us. Sin separates man from God. Jesus' death removed this separation so that we can be close to God. At the moment our sin was placed upon Jesus, a separation occurred. It had never happened before, and it will never happen again. There was a pause in an eternal union. This was the most painful aspect of what Jesus went through. He experienced for a few moments on the cross what the first Adam had experienced after his failure in the garden—an absence of the Father's presence. *And at the ninth hour Jesus cried out with a loud voice, saying, "Eloi, Eloi, lama sabachthani?" which is translated, "My God, My God, why have You forsaken Me?" And Jesus cried out with a loud voice, and breathed His last* (Mk 15:34, 37). Like a little boy in trouble cries out, "Where's Daddy?", Jesus cries out for the presence of His Father. At that one incredible moment when our sins were placed on Jesus, Father God had to distance Himself.

When Adam sinned, he felt the guilt of personal sin and wanted to hide from Father God. He took leaves off a tree and covered himself. However, Jesus, who did not commit personal sin, but chose to bear our sin for us, was still crying out for His *Daddy* as He died. He was not hiding from God. He was looking for God. This is the power of righteousness—to be able to look for God in the middle of your most unbearable moment knowing that He is all you will need.

Unlike Adam who ran and hid from God and covered himself with leaves, Jesus hung uncovered on a leafless tree looking for His Father. He is not hiding, but Father is. Father could rescue Him, but He doesn't. Why? God turned away from His Son for a moment so that He would not have to turn away from us forever. Jesus was willing to be forsaken so that we would not have to be. Because of what Jesus did on the cross, no true son or daughter of God will ever again face a moment when God turns away. We have His promise that He will never leave us or forsake us! *...For He Himself has said, "I will never leave you nor forsake you"* (He 13:5).

When the first Adam sinned, Father came looking for him. His heart was not to rid Himself of Adam because Adam had sinned.

His heart was to redeem him because he had sinned. He immediately took steps to position Adam to be able to live a long life, though death would ultimately come. He sacrificed an animal and covered Adam and Eve with its skin. This was a picture of the future day when He would cover sinful man with the blood of His own Son. This shows us Father's heart. He came to Adam and Eve in their sin to provide them a way out. Ultimately, He came as a man, Jesus, the last Adam, to lead us all the way out.

"Daddy, where are you?" is the cry deep within every human heart. As Jesus hung on the cross, the sins of all humanity were placed upon Him. When He cried out, *Father, Father, why have you forsaken me?*, He was asking the question that all humanity is asking, "God, where are you?" This question always arises when we are trapped under the fogbank of sin. "Where did you go, God? Why did you bail out on me?" When Jesus said, *Why have you forsaken me?*, it was the first and only time Jesus ever questioned the Father. He had always lived in complete subjection and obedience to the Father, but on the cross, when He was carrying our sin, He felt something He had never felt—the absence of His Father's presence. At that moment, He truly entered into the experience of sinful man as He felt what the first Adam felt—death was working in Him. He entered into death that He might bring us back to life. Suspended between heaven and earth on a tree of torture, the sinless Son of God experienced isolation and separation as the shroud of darkness covered the earth. What a dark day it was! What a bright day it has become!

During my senior year of high school, my dad opened a small underground coal mine. He had been an underground miner in his younger days and tried to make a go of it again. It didn't work out for him because there was too much water and the rock top was too soft. During the time it was operating, I worked a few days during the summer before my college classes started. The mine consisted of three shafts that had been dug horizontally into the side of a hill. The middle shaft was the one where a huge shaker pan was set up to vibrate the coal from inside the mines to the outside. I crawled on my stomach several hundred feet back into the mine. The clearance from the floor to the ceiling was a mere 30 inches. I remember lying on my side and shoveling coal into the shaker pan. It was really hard work. Firewood timbers were wedged between the ground and the ceiling to keep the ceiling from caving in. We wore hard helmets and battery belt packs that powered a headlamp. This furnished the light to see in the mines. I remember turning off my headlamp while deep inside the mine. It was the darkest dark I have ever seen. There was no trace or hint of light to be seen. I remember the fear of being lost and alone sweeping through my emotions. I quickly switched my headlamp back on and was happy to see that solid shaft of light shining wherever I turned my head. While on the cross, Jesus had no headlamp. He hung there in utter darkness, though He was the light of the world. What a stark contrast this was to the experience He had earlier, when He was transfigured on the mountaintop lit by the glory of God before His disciples. While on the cross, on a different mountain, there was only darkness. Our sin covered Him and darkness covered the earth. How utterly alone He must have felt.

Jesus had never existed in a place or a time when He was not fully aware of the Father's presence. At the cross, however, there were those moments when He entered into the place that the fallen first Adam and all his descendents had been living since the days of Eden. During this time, He became sin, not through an act of evil but through an act of love. Enduring this separation prepared the way for our restoration. This was what Jesus came to do—restore us to the place the first Adam left.

The place of intimate closeness to Father God is what every yearning heart unknowingly desires. Jesus taught that He came from the bosom of the Father, but during those moments on the cross before His death, the arms of Father God were not around Him. This is what sin does. It makes us feel outside Father's embrace. This is what happened to the first Adam. He had awakened in the bosom of the Father, but sin drove Him away from the embrace for which he was made.

The first Adam opened his eyes in the first moment and saw the face of God. Jesus, the last Adam, spent His last moments and breathed His last breath unable to see the face of God. Jesus could not see the Father, and the Father could not see Jesus. During this darkness, the wrath of God for you and me was poured out on Jesus. He suffered for us. He died for us. He endured the most ignominious death possible, so we could have the honor of being sons and daughters of God.

Forsake is translated from the Greek word, *egkataleípœ*. According to *The Complete Word Study Dictionary: New Testament*, it means, "to leave behind in any place or state." In other words, Jesus felt left behind. Is this not what sin does to the human race? We feel left behind. We tend to see God walking away from us. This is not true. Adam and Eve, because of their sin, walked away from God. They went and hid. They covered themselves.

Has God left us? No! We have left Him. Did God immediately remove Himself from Adam and Eve when they sinned? No! He came to them and covered them. He declared the results of the curse that sin brought upon humankind. He also declared judgment upon the serpent and in doing so gave Adam and Eve a future and a hope that a child would be born who would crush the serpent's head. *And I will put enmity between you and the woman, and between your seed and her Seed; he shall bruise your head, and you shall bruise His heel* (Ge 3:15).

It was not Father God who withdrew from them; they withdrew from Him. Are there not times in the lives of God's redeemed children when it seems that He cannot be found? Does this mean He is not present? Or, does it mean that we cannot feel His presence? Wasn't it the prodigal who left home? Wasn't the Father waiting when he returned? The weeping Father ran to meet his son and fell upon his neck covering him with kisses.

What would have happened had the first Adam offered himself for his bride Eve when she sinned? Would it have been possible at that moment for the perfect man to offer to bear the judgment for the sin of his now imperfect wife? Instead, he chose to enter into sin with her. *Then the eyes of both of them were opened, and they knew that they were naked; and they sewed fig leaves together and made themselves coverings* (Ge 3:7).

In Genesis 2:7, Adam's eyes were opened to see God. In Genesis 3:7, his eyes were opened to see evil. In between these two chapters was an act of disobedience that caused man and woman to turn away from everything they would ever need to pursue the one thing they were never supposed to have. They hid themselves from Father. This is still happening every day across the world. We see the great heart of our loving Heavenly Father pursuing His children who are pursuing sin. Eve blamed the serpent. Adam blamed Eve. He blamed God for giving him Eve. We certainly are all children of Adam because we still blame the devil, our spouse, and God for our sin.

The last Adam, Jesus, chose not to enter into sin but to offer Himself for our sin. He gave Himself for His bride. Though He was not to blame, He willingly took the blame. Martin Luther sums it up, "Either sin is with you, lying on your shoulders, or it is lying on Christ, the Lamb of God. Now if it is lying on your back, you are lost; but if it is resting on Christ, you are free, and you will be saved. Now choose what you want." Because of what Jesus did, we can have the hope that when we breathe our last breath, we will open our eyes in the paradise of another world, see the face of God, and experience His presence forever.

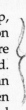

FOURTEEN

THE REVELATION OF BELONGING

Never be afraid to trust an unknown future to a known God.
Corrie Ten Boom

Loneliness is a powerful emotion. Being alone can be invigorating for a little while. We all need some alone time. But being lonely and being alone are two different issues. We were created to belong. The cosmos is a lonely place if you do not know where you truly belong. There are many men and women wearing business suits, driving luxury automobiles, surrounded by all the trappings of success who are orphans. They have lots of papers describing what belongs to them, but their hearts tell them that they still have not done enough to really be happy. Much of the drive that has contributed to their worldly success can be attributed to their need to belong to something that is bigger than they are. They have an inner yearning for that elusive something or someone in the regions beyond. They are lonely. You can be alone and have great contentment. Yet, you can be with a crowd of people and still be under the suffocating chokehold of loneliness. You were not created to be alone or lonely. You were created to be with God and belong to Him. By the way, you do not have to own the luxury car or wear a business suit to struggle with loneliness. You just have to be without the revelation of who you were created to be. The revelation

85

that you were created to be a son or daughter of God provides the missing key to understanding what life is all about. Everything needed to withstand the schemes of Satan against your life, family, job, or ministry is available to God's children. In general terms, all of humanity are God's children by virtue of creation; however, it is when you are adopted into God's family through redemption that you receive the divine credential of being God's child. When you receive Jesus, you receive sonship. Have you received Jesus?

But as many as received Him, to them He gave the right to become children of God, to those who believe in His name… (Jo 1:12). It was in the heart of God to create sons and daughters so that He could enjoy them as they enjoyed Him forever. After the fall of man, his fellowship with God was broken. God immediately began moving in redemption to restore man back to the place he had forfeited. As you continue to read the book of Genesis, you discover that God called a man to become the father of a new nation of people. The man whom God called was named Abram. The children of Abraham were to be a special people to God. This people would be the people through whom the Messiah would come. The Messiah would be the Savior of mankind. He would be the one to redeem man, restoring him back into a close intimate relationship with God.

When God called Abram, He changed his name to Abraham, meaning "father of many nations." God wanted Abraham to have sons and daughters who would cover the earth with the truth of who the real God was and is. By changing his name to Abraham, God found a man who would reflect in the earth what He was carrying in His heart. God wanted Abraham to be a father of many nations because that is what God carried in His heart—the desire to be Father to sons and daughters of the nations of the world. Abraham, who was well along in years and without a child of his own, stepped faithfully into the destiny that God had placed before him.

We see in the heart of God the desire to be a Father to all the nations. So the Old Testament was established on God's desire to have sons and daughters throughout the nations. Abraham would be the forerunner preparing the way for many sons and daughters to have a special relationship with God. God always raises up forerunners to birth the message of the Father-Son relationship because it keeps getting lost. You can trace this throughout the Bible.

Yet there was also a constant struggle between fathers and sons. When you go back to the beginning, the heart of God was for the father/son relationship to be the place where the anointing of the Holy Spirit was to abide. The Holy Spirit was present when Adam was created to fellowship with his Heavenly Father. The Holy Spirit is present today at every occasion when a son or daughter comes home to their Heavenly Father.

When Jesus came, He demonstrated for us how a Son is to live and honor the Father and how the Father honors and nurtures the Son. He has gone before us preparing the way for us to have relationship with our Heavenly Father. Jesus pioneered the way for us to follow. God raises up forerunners to pioneer and restore. There are forerunners being raised up in our day to prepare the people for the coming of the Lord. Among other truths, the forerunner carries a message that calls for the restoration of the father/son–father/daughter relationship.

The old covenant closes with the following declarative promise concerning a messenger carrying a message of restoration: *Behold, I will send you Elijah the prophet before the coming of the great and dreadful day of the LORD. And he will turn the hearts of the fathers to the children, And the hearts of the children to their fathers, Lest I come and strike the earth with a curse* (Mal 4:5-6).

Zacharias and Elizabeth were told that their son was to be named John, and he would come in the spirit and power of Elijah. He also was identified as the messenger promised in Malachi 3:1: *"Behold, I send My messenger, and he will prepare the way before Me. And the Lord, whom you seek, will suddenly come to His temple, even the Messenger of the covenant, in whom you delight. Behold, He is coming,"* says the LORD *of hosts.* John was the forerunner for the first coming of Jesus. I cover this in detail in my book, *The Forerunner Anointing.* John came to announce the arrival of Jesus—the Messiah. Jesus came to restore the broken relationship that existed between Father God and His children here on the earth.

God wants to restore the hearts of the fathers to the children and the children to the fathers because that is what God meant when He started the old covenant and changed Abram's name to Abraham. God's design and His desire are global. He wants everybody everywhere to get on board the family-of-God train, which is heading for glory. He has commissioned the church to take the Gospel to all the nations because He loves all people and wants them to be saved.

Jesus came to save us but also to show us how to walk in relationship with the Father. Jesus' baptism in the Jordan River marked the beginning of His public ministry. He started with a big "I'm proud of you, Son!" given to Him by His Father. The heavens opened overhead. The Holy Spirit came down in the form of a dove and lit upon Jesus. Then the Father affirmed His Son with the powerful words that every child yearns to hear, *"This is My beloved Son, in whom I am well pleased"* (Ma 3:17).

It is so important for a believer to know who he or she is. The next day after His baptism, Jesus entered the wilderness to be tempted by the devil. He fasted for forty days, and then the devil came to tempt Him. How did he tempt Him? He targeted Jesus' identity. He tried to get Jesus to prove who He was. If Jesus had tried to prove who He was to the devil, He would have denied who He was before His Father. Repeatedly, *If you are the son of God...* (Ma 4) was the question that Satan dared Jesus to prove. Jesus stood strong. He did not have to prove it. Father had already told Him. He *knew* who He was.

The first Adam failed because he did not hold to what His Father said concerning who he was. Adam sinned because he wanted to be somebody different. He wanted to become as God. Adam was already God's son. He was already made in God's image. Jesus, the last Adam, refused to prove who He knew He was. When you *know* who you are, you do not have to *prove* who you are.

The Father gave Jesus this revelation of Sonship and affirmation for two reasons. First, He meant it. He loved Jesus and was pleased with what He was doing. Second, He knew Jesus would need it. God doesn't give us a revelation just so we can say we have heard something from God. He gives it to us because He knows what is coming around the curve. He sends words that will strengthen us for our successes and our storms.

The revelation that we are God's sons and daughters is the single revelation that will help us properly enjoy our successes and endure our storms. Oh, how we need to know who we are! Knowing who we are will keep us from trying to impress others or prove ourselves to them. How much trouble do we cook up by trying to prove who we are? In the family of God, it is hard to view others as brothers and sisters if we are not confident in the fact that we are sons and daughters.

Through faith in Christ, we are God's children. Father wants us to be convinced of this. The revelation of being God's child will keep you strong in the face of Satan's schemes. This is the single revelation that the Father gave Jesus as He began His public ministry and as He headed toward the cross. It was given to Jesus again on the Mount of Transfiguration when the glory of God, which was always in Jesus, was allowed to shine forth. Moses and Elijah appeared to Him and spoke with Him about His coming death. Again, Father God spoke from heaven saying, *This is my beloved Son, in whom I am well pleased.* Father knew that the cross would be the greatest storm Jesus would ever have to endure. He knew His Son would once again be tested to *prove* who He was or to *forget* who He was.

And those who passed by blasphemed Him, wagging their heads and saying ... "If You are the Son of God, come down from the cross" (Ma 27:39-40). Whether it was Satan or men, Jesus refused to prove who He was. He knew who He was. He handled Satan and the crowd, but the one thing that was almost unbearable to Him was being forsaken by His Father. The evil that was present in all our sins created a dark cloud between Father and Son. This was witnessed in the natural on the day of the crucifixion: *Now it was about the sixth hour, and there was darkness over all the earth until the ninth hour. Then the sun was darkened, and the veil of the temple was torn in two. And when Jesus had cried out with a loud voice, He said, "Father, 'into Your hands I commit My spirit.'"* Having said this, He breathed His last (Lk 23:44-46).

There was darkness over the whole Earth for a three-hour period during the crucifixion. The sun was darkened. In those three hours of darkness, He suffered an eternity of agony so that we could spend an eternity in liberty. Though Jesus had cried out that God had forsaken Him, He still had faith that His Father would take care of Him on the other side of death. He died trusting Father with His last breath. He died knowing He was God's son because He died calling God His Father. He held to the revelation though He could not see the face of God nor hear the voice of God. It was the only time that there ever was or ever will be a pause in the sweet fellowship that Jesus so enjoys with His Father. The Father turned away from Jesus for a few moments so that He would not have to turn away from us forever.

The last breath out of the last Adam was a cry of submission to the Father. From the first breath to the last breath, we are to pursue the presence of the Father. This is our destiny. When you know who your Father is, then you know whose child you are. Jesus died yielding His spirit to His Father. In the midst of bearing the sins of all mankind, He held to the revelation that He was Father's beloved son.

When we read to the end of the Bible, we see people gathered together from all around the world standing before the throne of God worshipping Him. In Revelation 7, we see the representation of His sons and daughters gathered together from all the nations. They are there from all the ethnic groups and people groups from around the globe. He is the Father of all the nations. *After these things I looked, and behold, a great multitude which no one could number, of all nations, tribes, peoples, and tongues, standing before the throne and before the Lamb, clothed with white robes, with palm branches in their hands, and crying out with a loud voice, saying, "Salvation* belongs *to our God who sits on the throne, and to the Lamb!"* (Re 7:9-10).

God put Adam and Eve in the Garden to be bearers of His glory— to reflect His image in the earth. He commanded them to be fruitful and multiply. It is as if He were saying, "I want this Earth filled with My sons and My daughters." Before the end comes, the desire of Father God will be realized in the realm of Earth. The church is not going to limp out of here whining on her way to heaven. A pure church will be caught up in glorious victory. God is not going to go down in defeat. Before it is all over, this earth will be filled with the glory of the Lord as the seas are covered by water. He will receive praise from sons and daughters all across the earth.

The earth itself is groaning, waiting for the children of God to be revealed in their glorious liberty. Paul wrote about this in his letter to the Roman believers. *For the earnest expectation of the creation eagerly waits for the revealing of the sons of God. For the creation was subjected to futility, not willingly, but because of Him who subjected* it *in hope; because the creation itself also will be delivered from the bondage of corruption into the glorious liberty of the children of God* (Ro 8:19-21). When God placed Adam in the Garden of Eden, He gave him and Eve dominion in the earth. There is a sense in which Adam was lord over the earth. He was given authority by his Father God to rule over all the created order. Everything was subject to him in the realm of Earth. I believe that everything responded positively to Adam before the fall. He worked, but it was not laborious. All of his efforts were 100 percent productive. The power of the curse was not working against him. The Spirit of God upon his life caused everything to respond to him with favor. He had the God-given capacity to multiply, explore, and reign as God's regent in the realm of the earth. The animals were subject to him. Not one of them desired Adam for lunch. There was no aggression, anger, or animosity to cause disharmony in the natural order of things.

The disharmony started when Adam and Eve, who were the highest authorities in the earth, stepped away from God, who was their authority. Through faith in Jesus Christ and the power of the cross, we are once again authorized to be children of God in the realm of Earth. *But as many as received Him, to them He gave the right to become children of God, to those who believe in His name* (Jo 1:12).

FATHER'S HOME IN YOU

FIFTEEN

HOLY SPIRIT, COME!

*The preaching that this world needs most
is the sermons in shoes that are walking with Jesus Christ.*

D. L. Moody

The first human body was made to be a dwelling place for the Spirit of God. God filled Adam with His own Spirit. This is the way God intended for man to live his life—full of the Spirit of God. The Bible teaches us to live this way. In Ephesians 3:19, the Apostle Paul prayed for believers to *be filled with all the fullness of God.* Later in Ephesians 5:18, he commanded them to *be filled with the Spirit.* We are to be filled, and we are to *stay full* of the Spirit.

I recently listened to an old recording of Dr. C. L. Culpepper in which he recounted some of his recollections of the 1920s revival in Shantung, China. As a missionary, he and his associates were burdened to see souls saved in China. There were some older missionaries who knew how to pray, and they had been seeking God earnestly for revival. Some of the younger ones left due to the difficulty of the work. Times were tough, and the work was hard.

Prior to the harvest, he and other missionaries went through a four-year period when God dealt with them about getting the "rubbish" out of their lives. During this time, a Lutheran missionary from Norway, Marie Munsen, asked him, "Brother Culpepper, have you been filled with the Holy Spirit?" He responded, "I don't know because I don't understand what it means." He and others were convicted of their need to know what it meant and to be filled with the Holy Spirit. He stated, "I felt like God would kill me if I did not get an understanding of the fullness of the Holy Spirit." He began facing the fear of the excesses he had read about, the fear of being misunderstood by his denomination, and the fear of certain manifestations. One week after four days of continual praise and prayer with about forty others had concluded, he and two other men desperate for breakthrough drew away to continue to seek God. He threw up his hands and prayed, "Lord, I want all you have for me." This precious man of God said, "My mouth was open wide and it felt like the wind of all the world rushed down my throat." He described the feeling like a thousand magnets drawing him from all sides. He stated that God was shaking him like a dog shaking a rabbit. He was overwhelmed by the presence and power of the Holy Spirit. He wept. He laughed. He shook. His heart and body literally throbbed under the presence and power of the Holy Spirit. He testified that he became a changed man and the evidence that followed backs him up. In answer to the prayers of these burdened missionaries, God began to visit through the power of His Spirit and their eyes were allowed to see a mighty move of God in the Shantung Province that resulted in the salvation of many thousands of Chinese souls. It takes power to see souls saved, and we serve a God of power. We need to be full of His Holy Spirit. I am not talking about a doctrinal concept, but a living reality. We all need to arrive at the point where we pray in agreement with Brother Culpepper, "Lord, I want all you have for me." You and I were made to be full of the Spirit of God.[11]

Solomon's Temple had an outer court, the holy place, and the holy of holies. This represented man who is body, soul, and spirit. The holy of holies represented a man's spirit. It was within the holy of holies that the glory of the Spirit of God would reside. God always intended to dwell within man through His Spirit. Man's body was represented by the outer court. Man's soul was represented by the holy place. Ezekiel wrote of the temple where the glory had departed—this is what a man is without the Spirit of God within him. He is empty of the life of God for which he was made. The presence of God does not fill his life.

When the Lord created Adam, He placed His Spirit inside Adam's spirit. When Adam stood to his feet for the first time, he stood as a perfect man filled with the Spirit of God. "Filled with the

Spirit" is the way man was made to live. This was the way Jesus lived. This is the way that you are designed and destined to live. The Apostle Paul explained what happens to the person whose life is lived through the Holy Spirit: *For as many as are led by the Spirit of God, these are sons of God. For you did not receive the spirit of bondage again to fear, but you received the Spirit of adoption by whom we cry out, "Abba, Father." The Spirit Himself bears witness with our spirit that we are children of God* . . . (Ro 8:14-16). The Holy Spirit leads us. The Holy Spirit frees us. The Holy Spirit bears witness that we have been adopted into God's family as His children. The word *abba* means "father" or "daddy." It means that we relate to the Almighty God of this universe as His little kids. Isn't this just absolutely wonderful?

The most primitive cry of the human heart is "Daddy." When the Spirit of God comes to live in us, the relationship with God as Father is established, and the deep yearning of our heart is satisfied with His love and affection.

Before Jesus began His ministry, John the Baptist, the forerunner, was proclaiming that Jesus would impact people with the ministry of the Holy Spirit. *I indeed baptize you with water unto repentance, but He who is coming after me is mightier than I, whose sandals I am not worthy to carry. He will baptize you with the Holy Spirit and fire* (Ma 3:11). It was like John was saying, "When He gets here, the Holy Spirit is going to impact your life. You are going to have encounters with the Holy Spirit." This signaled that God would once again breathe on His children with His Spirit and awaken them to the life He intended them to have in the beginning. We were made for God to breathe on us and fill us with His Holy Spirit. Jesus' ministry was marked by the presence of power of the Holy Spirit. He intended for His followers to minister in the same way.

Prior to His ascension, Jesus gathered His disciples together and commissioned them. He wanted to send them forth just as He had been sent forth. He then breathed the breath of God on them. *And when He had said this, He breathed on* them, *and said to them, "Receive the Holy Spirit"* (Jo 20:22). He still desires to breathe on His disciples today. Have you experienced the breath of God upon your life through the Holy Spirit?

On the day of Pentecost, God poured out His Spirit once again upon His children. The sound of a rushing, mighty wind filled the place where praying believers waited on the promise of the Father.

They were all filled with the Holy Spirit. Isn't it interesting that people from all the nations were there? This must have made Father God very happy. When this happened, the Apostle Peter recognized it as the fulfillment of the Old Testament prophecy of Joel. *And it shall come to pass in the last days, says God, That I will pour out of My Spirit on all flesh; Your sons and your daughters shall prophesy, Your young men shall see visions, Your old men shall dream dreams* (Ac 2:17). Jesus' death on the cross made it possible for man and woman to have the Holy Spirit poured out upon them once again.

In the Spirit, we are sons and daughters of God as believers in Jesus Christ. His Holy Spirit working through us energizes us to live for Father. We need God's breath in our lives in order to live the life He intends for us. We should welcome and not resist the move of His Spirit in and through our lives. We cannot accomplish what needs to be accomplished without the Holy Spirit. It just will not happen.

I have a pastor friend who testified the Lord spoke to him while he was in seminary completing his doctor of ministry degree. In the middle of the library surrounded by tens of thousands of books containing the best teaching on ministry that man can offer, the Lord whispered to him and said, "Your ministry is of the Holy Spirit, or it is nothing." Of course, this surprised my friend. Why would the Lord say such a thing to him personally if there were not a need for him to make a correction? So, he started studying about the Holy Spirit. As a result, he now has a ministry that is truly led by the Holy Spirit. He is able to see God do things that he used to only read about in the Bible. The Holy Spirit was not just for the days of the Bible. He is for here and now.

We must be careful not to allow our traditions to keep us from being open to the power and ministry of the Holy Spirit operating in our lives. As mentioned earlier, John the Baptist taught his disciples that the ministry of the Messiah would be marked by the ministry of the Holy Spirit. Did you know that some of them lost this precious truth in one generation? In Acts 19, Paul met some of John's disciples in Ephesus. It was about 20-25 years after John had been beheaded and Jesus had been crucified. Notice what these followers of John's teaching said in response to a question from Paul concerning the Holy Spirit: *He said to them, "Did you receive the Holy Spirit when you believed?" So they said to him, "We have not so much as heard whether there is a Holy Spirit." And he said to them, "Into what then were you baptized?" So they said, "Into John's baptism"* (Ac 19:2-3).

These men had been instructed by other followers of John. They had been baptized as John had commanded, but the message of the Holy Spirit had been lost. They testified that they did not even know there *was* a Holy Spirit. The ministry of the Holy Spirit was at the core of what John the Baptist had preached about Jesus. Yet, in one generation, some of his followers had let this important teaching slip away from them. They held to the methods of what John did, but they did not hold to the full message that John preached. Paul, however, quickly taught them about the full message of Jesus and the empowerment of the Holy Spirit. As soon as they heard, they were baptized in Jesus' name. Paul laid hands on them, and they were filled with the Holy Spirit. They even spoke in tongues as the disciples had done on the day of Pentecost. By the way, don't be sidetracked by how the Holy Spirit may manifest in someone's life. Too much strife has taken place over the manifestations of the Holy Spirit. Let the Holy Spirit do what He wants to do in your life! Your body is His temple; let Him use it as He wills. It is the fruit of your life after a manifestation that tells the story of what really happened. The fruit itself is the manifestation we should be after.

My own life and ministry have been greatly changed due to an encounter with the Holy Spirit. I was a successful pastor with a fairly large congregation. I loved Jesus, prayed, witnessed, and studied the Word of God. On paper, I had most of things that I had dreamed of attaining as a pastor. A good salary, nice home, country club amenities, status in the community, and a loving church family were all part of my life. However, in the midst of ministry, I had become miserable. Desperation seized my soul and would not release me from the gnawing pain that there had to be more to life and ministry than I was experiencing. Too much of what I was doing could be attributed to what I was doing. During this season of desperation, the Lord began dealing with me about the motives of my heart. I came to realize that much of what I was doing was for man's approval. I found myself reading the Book of Acts in wonder at the power that flowed through the early church. It was so evident that there was a power in the early church that was not present in much of today's church. There was a power in the early disciples that I did not witness in my own life. To them, it was not about programs and methods; it was about power and ministry. The Holy

Spirit worked through them in undeniable ways. Much of what they did could only be explained by the power of God. Little of what I did could be attributed to the power of God.

Finally, I came to the breaking point. I caught myself thinking one day about not doing ministry anymore. I needed a touch from God. I needed what the early church had. I am so grateful that the Lord heard my desperate cry for more. Space does not allow for all the details, but the Lord visited me through the power of the Holy Spirit. A dear man who knew of the power of the Holy Spirit was used by the Lord to help me. He prayed for me. I had never experienced such power in all my life. It was like waves of electrical energy coursing through my body. I was overwhelmed by the presence of God. I could hardly walk afterwards. For several days, my body trembled as if it were vibrating. From that moment on, my life and ministry have been remarkably different. Prayer became so refreshing. I wanted to read the Bible more than ever, and it began coming alive as never before. I started hearing the voice of the Holy Spirit speaking to my heart in powerful ways.

Since that night, I have witnessed the Holy Spirit at work doing that which is impossible with man. God breathed on me, and my life was changed. I have had dreams in which I received divine direction. I have seen Jesus heal people from sickness and disease. I have seen Jesus set people free who were caught in Satan's traps. I have witnessed Jesus at work in so many powerful ways that I did not see before. All of this started after I became so desperate that I could not go on without the power of the Holy Spirit in my life. "Christian" is more than a label we wear; it should reflect Christ living through our lives.

I have read of many great men of God who have had such experiences with the Holy Spirit. D. L. Moody, who was a famous evangelist of a past generation, was used by the Lord to shake nations. Read the following testimony in which he describes a change he experienced when the Holy Spirit came upon him:

"When I was preaching in Farwell Hall, in Chicago, I never worked harder to prepare my sermons than I did then. I preached and preached; but it was beating against the air. A good woman used to say, 'Mr. Moody, you don't seem to have power in your preaching.' Oh, my desire was that I might have a fresh anointing. I requested this woman and a few others to come and pray with me every Friday at four o'clock. Oh, how piteously I prayed that God might fill the empty vessel. After the fire in Chicago, I was in New York City and going into the bank on Wall Street, it seemed as if I felt a strange and mighty power coming over me. I went up to the hotel, and there in my room I wept before God, and cried, 'Oh, my God, stay Thy hand!' He gave me such fullness that it seemed more than I could contain. May God forgive me if I should speak in a boastful way, but I do not know that I have preached a sermon since, but God has given me some soul. Oh, I would not be back where I was four years ago for all the wealth of this world. If you would roll it at my feet, I would kick it away like a football. I seem a wonder to some of you, but I am a greater wonder to myself than to any one else. These are the very same sermons I preached in Chicago, word for word. It is not new sermons, but the power of God. It is not a new gospel, but the old gospel, with the Holy Ghost of power."[12]

People call experiences such as these by different names: baptism of the Holy Spirit, being filled with the Spirit, the fullness of God, or being endued with power from on high. These are all biblical terms that can be used. Don't argue about what to call it—just get it! When the wind from heaven blows upon you, you will be changed. When people are saved, the Holy Spirit comes to live "within" them—this is awesome! There are also times when the Holy Spirit moves upon people to empower them to do something. This is the "upon" you ministry of the Holy Spirit. One has to do with salvation, and the other has to do with serving God. The Holy Spirit will give us what we need in every circumstance so that we can do what God wants us to do. This giving to us is always a grace gift. It comes from Him and does not originate with us. We are to serve God through the power of the Holy Spirit. If we do not, then we are serving Him through our own strength. This is where misery is made. Too many children of God are tired and frustrated because they are serving God in their own strength. When God breathes upon a person with the power of His Holy Spirit, what was drudgery becomes delight. You and I were created to function under the anointing of the Holy Spirit!

We all love and respect Dr. Billy Graham. I was recently reading a new book about his leadership skills. Early in the book, authors Harold Myra and Marshall Shelly record the story of Graham being filled with the Holy Spirit. Many years ago while in the British Isles, he met an evangelist named Stephen Olford. Olford was a young man at the time, but eventually became very well known for his passion, power, and excellence in expository preaching. Upon hearing Stephen Olford preach about being filled with the Holy Spirit, Billy Graham was deeply moved and wanted to hear more about the subject. This inquiry resulted in Olford setting aside two days to spend in a small hotel with Billy Graham. During the day, Stephen Olford would share from the word with Billy Graham and then at night they attended services where Billy was preaching. After the first night's message, Stephen Olford recounted that Billy's preaching was "very ordinary," having little impact on the people. Back at the room, Olford shared of the brokenness that he had gone through in his journey to becoming filled with "fullness and anointing." Let me share a section from the book with you:

"I gave him my testimony of how God completely turned my life inside out—an experience of the Holy Spirit in his fullness and anointing," said Olford. "As I talked, and I can see him now, those marvelous eyes glistened with tears, and he said, 'Stephen, I see it. That's what I want. That's what I need in my life.'" Olford suggested they "pray this through," and both men knelt on the floor.

"I can still hear Billy pouring out his heart in a prayer of total dedication to the Lord," said Olford. "Finally, he said, 'My heart is so flooded with the Holy Spirit!', and we went from praying to praising. We were laughing and praising God, and Billy was walking back and forth across the room, crying out, 'I have it! I'm filled. This is the turning point in my life.' And he was a new man."

As Billy recalls the experience years later, "I was beginning to understand that Jesus himself was our victory, through the Holy Spirit's power."

That night, when Billy preached, "for reasons known only to God alone, the place which was only moderately filled the night before was packed to the doors," said Olford. "As Billy rose to speak, he was a man absolutely anointed."

Members of the audience came forward to pray even before Billy gave an invitation. At the end of the sermon, practically the entire crowd rushed forward.

"My own heart was so moved by Billy's authority and strength that I could hardly drive home," Olford remembers. "When I came in the door, my father looked at my face and said, 'What on earth happened?' I sat down at the kitchen table and said, 'Dad, something has happened to Billy Graham. The world is going to hear from this man.'"[13]

This account of Stephen Olford, affirmed by Billy Graham himself, is powerful and very meaningful, especially in light of the caliber of these two great men of God. I personally had the privilege of studying under Dr. Olford while working on my doctoral studies in expository preaching. He was a passionate prince of preachers who left his mark for Jesus Christ on the world through his anointed ministry. As to Billy Graham, no one can deny that people around the globe respect him for the many years of godly living and preaching the gospel. I remember being in the World Congress Center in Atlanta, Georgia on an occasion that Dr. Graham came and spoke to the Southern Baptist Convention. When he walked into the building, you could feel the atmosphere in the place shift. The awe of God filled my soul in an unusual way. What was this? It was the presence of God working through the presence of a man. Billy Graham's humility and authority are characteristics that no one can deny. Millions have heard about Jesus through the voice of Billy Graham. On the threshold of those two life-changing days prior to his meeting in that small hotel, he told Stephen Olford, "You've spoken of something that I don't have. I want the fullness of the Holy Spirit in my life too."[14] May the Lord hear this prayer of desire arising from all of our hearts.

Jesus, in many ways, instructs us of our need to be rooted in Him so that His power and authority can operate in our lives. John records for us Jesus' words to His disciples spoken shortly before He went to the cross: *I am the vine, you are the branches. He who abides in Me, and I in him, bears much fruit; for without Me you can do nothing* (Jo 15:5).

It is the precious presence of the Holy Spirit moving and flowing through our lives that releases the fragrance of Jesus Christ into the nostrils of the hurting world surrounding us. Ask your Heavenly Father to breathe on you right now. Seek Him while knowing that He desires to fill you and empower you to do His will. It takes power to live righteously in this present world! It takes power to overcome the pressures of the system of this world that wars against the soul. Power is necessary to break out of the bondages that entangle the human heart with sin and defeat. Before the fall, Adam was full of the Spirit, and the whole earth was subjected to him. Through the power of the Spirit of God operating in his life, he exercised dominion. All creation was under his feet. He was God's regent in the realm of Earth. After his fall into sin, things radically changed. A war now exists that did not exist before the fall. The creation is under the power of the curse. Man has to war against the weeds. He has to war against predators. He has to war against other men. He wars against sickness and death. He wars against poverty and famine. He has a war waging inside of him as well. It certainly takes power to rise above all this to live life the way God intends. We need the power of God's breath upon us to win the war. It takes power to win wars! Oh! We desperately need the Spirit of God residing within us to live for God, and we need the Spirit of God flowing through us to do the will and work of God. Come, Holy Spirit and fill our lives!

SIXTEEN

LIVING THE INSPIRED LIFE

꧁ᆖ꩓

Everyone who believes in God at all
believes that He knows
what you and I are going to do tomorrow.

C. S. Lewis

At the time of this writing, my wife and I have been married for 28 years. We were mere babes at 18 and 19 years of age when we exchanged our vows. God has been good to us. Mikki finished college and got a job teaching elementary school, and I was working as an industrial carpenter before our third anniversary rolled around. With her first paycheck, we decided to celebrate. We bought her a new mini-sized dishwasher for our mobile home, and I was able to buy a new acoustic guitar. I thought I would be a guitar star. I started taking bluegrass guitar lessons. In addition to being a guitar star, I thought I might be a songwriter as well. I wrote a lot of unknown hits that were off the charts—way off, like, completely out of sight! However, there was one song I wrote that got some notice from my wife. I wrote a song about her. I was 23 and in love. I titled it, "You're My Inspiration!" I would strum the strings of my guitar, look into her eyes, and sing my song of love to her. It's funny now to think of what I knew about success at age 23. The first verse and chorus went like this:

I've got everything in life,
That a man could possibly ever want
Success was a dream I fulfilled a long time ago.
I could take the credit,
But I won't.
I owe it all to the one that I love so.

You're my inspiration!
Every day with you is a rainbow's end.
You're my inspiration!
You're much more than a lover,
Much, much, more than a friend.

It makes you want to cry, doesn't it? A lot of my singing made people want to cry, if you know what I mean. I actually went around to a few smaller churches and sang songs and played my guitar. I was never invited back for repeat performances, so I would find a new audience and test their toleration level. I was to discover, slower than everyone else did, that I was not inspired to be a singer and songwriter. The exception was the private performances that I sang to my wife. When the Lord called me to preach, I think my wife and all the folks at church we attended were happy (and relieved) that I would be preaching and not singing. So, I had to settle for being a sanctified shower singer. I must admit, my preaching has been much closer to *inspirational* than my singing ever was. While I didn't become a guitar star—despite my efforts—I *did* gain a few brownie points from Mikki for singing my song to her. I also learned that when someone or something is inspired, other people notice it as well.

The words "inspire" and "expire" are used often in our everyday language. The meaning derived from their usage is linked to context. We speak of an artist who was inspired to paint a beautiful picture. We refer to a minister's inspiring sermon. The doctor shares the heartbreaking news that a loved one just expired. The police officer writes you a ticket because the time on your parking meter expired. Physiologically, *inspire* means "to breathe in" and *expire* means "to breathe out." In simple terms, the words mean *in* and *out*. One has to do with something that takes place within you. The other has to do with something that terminates or runs out.

Theologically, *inspire* means "to be under the influence of the

Spirit of God." One of the definitions in the fourth edition of *The American Heritage Dictionary* is "to affect, guide, or arouse by divine influence." With this in mind, as Adam drew in his first breath, his lungs were filled with the breath of God. He also became affected, guided, and aroused by the divine influence. He was created to live an inspired life, and so were you!

In a similar manner, the Scriptures arouse the reader with the power of the divine influence. Read what Paul wrote to Timothy concerning the Scripture: *All Scripture* is *given by inspiration of God, and* is *profitable for doctrine, for reproof, for correction, for instruction in righteousness...* (2 Ti 3:16). The word "inspiration" which Paul uses is the Greek word *theópneustos* meaning 'God-breathed.' The Bible is a book that came from the breath of God. Just as man was brought to life by the breath of God, the words of the Bible have been breathed on by the breath of God. This is the reason that the Bible has such a profound influence on a person who reads it with an open heart and mind. It agrees with what we carry deep in our DNA all the way back to Adam. It registers on our spirit because it originated from God's Spirit. Reading the Bible can cause a person to sense what Adam sensed when God first breathed on him. In this manner, the Bible is the word of life. Adam awoke and arose to hear the word of God and live an inspired life.

In the same way, God's word is profitable for us. As we read and obey, it aligns us with God Himself. Our beliefs are brought into alignment with God. Our behavior is brought into alignment with God. This alignment means we are corrected from unrighteousness to righteousness. This doesn't happen from reading the morning newspaper, but it does happen from reading the word of God. It is His word because He breathed it out to us. It proceeded from His mouth. It came from Him to us. When we inspire it, breathe it in, we become inspired by the Spirit of God. Wonderful things happen when we learn to speak the Word of God into our circumstances. When tempted by the devil, Jesus responded by speaking the Word of God into the situation. He overcame, and the devil fled away. The Word of God goes *out* of us after we have received it *into* us.

The Apostle Peter describes for us the activity of the Spirit of God upon a person through whom God speaks. *...for prophecy never came by the will of man, but holy men of God spoke* as they were *moved by the Holy Spirit* (2 Pe 1:21). The Holy Spirit moved the prophet to speak. The word "moved" has the idea of being carried or borne along by the Holy Spirit. Like wind carrying a sailboat across the water, the Spirit of God influences a person to speak the word of God. Most believers have had moments when they could feel the presence of the Holy Spirit moving them to share something with somebody. Occasions like this are moments of inspiration. Jesus taught that the Holy Spirit is like the wind. You cannot see the wind but you can see and feel its effects. *The wind blows where it wishes, and you hear the sound of it, but cannot tell where it comes from and where it goes. So is everyone who is born of the Spirit* (Jo 3:8).

Experiencing the new birth means God's Spirit has come to reside in your spirit. With the Holy Spirit living inside of you, there will be times when you will be carried places you had not planned to go, and you will be led to say things that you had not planned to say. When this happens, you feel the inspiration of the Holy Spirit upon your life. It is amazing what can happen in your life if you become sensitive to these promptings of the Holy Spirit. Jesus assured us that the Holy Spirit would be our helper. He taught us that the Holy Spirit would guide us into all truth. He also said the Holy Spirit would show us things to come. The Lord speaks to us in a variety of ways if only we will listen.

As you realize the Holy Spirit wants to provide inspiration in your life, you will have opportunities to see the creativity of God at work in your life. How many times have you heard a songwriter say a song was given to him or her like a file downloading to a computer? It is as if the thoughts became suspended and God's thoughts started rushing in. Most preachers have experienced a download of inspiration while preaching from the pulpit. When this happens, the whole audience can feel a shift in the atmosphere. They sense the presence of God in their midst working through the person ministering. Adam was created to walk in dominion. In a sense, this is what happens when we experience an inspired moment. A person hearing an inspired song or listening to an inspired sermon is able to transcend the difficulties in their life through what they are hearing. Hope is transferred to their hearts. Failure flees and peace comes. This is the work of the Spirit of God upon their lives. Power flows to remove obstacles and bring blessing.

This inspired guidance is onboard equipment for the child of God. Adam had this operating within him from the moment of his first breath. When God breathed into Adam, he experienced inspiration. We get it when we come to Father God through Jesus Christ and the Spirit of God breathes on us. We have been created to live supernatural lives. What an exciting idea that we can live inspired lives. As children of God, we are to be inspired until we expire.

I once read that the spire seen on top of a church building is linked to the idea of inspiration. Inspire means to breathe in. Spire means to breathe. So, a spire on a roof means the building is a place where the breath of God, the life of God, and the word of God goes out to the world. Every church should pray to be moved by the inspiration of God's Spirit. When people attend a church service, they should experience the life of God in the atmosphere. They should know that God is breathing on what is taking place. Going to a church service should be like going to a train station. It should carry you somewhere. Too often we have been content to wait in the lobby without ever boarding the glory train. Seriously, what makes the church different from other groups that get together to do something good? The church is to be sharing the good news that Jesus lives and our sins can be forgiven.

The architectural significance of a spire or steeple is that it points toward heaven. It symbolizes the church's connection to the world above. Haven't there been times when you were in a worship service and you sensed the presence of God stirring among the people? Don't you love it when you get to see and feel the effects of the wind blowing? I'm not just speaking of the stirring of your emotions; there is nothing wrong with that. I am speaking of the presence of God that you can sense in your spirit. Isn't it true, that as we gather to worship, our breath ascends in worship, and our spirits receive words that are sent from above? This expiring and inspiring is a picture of what is happening in the spiritual realm as we are led by the Spirit of God. There should be life among the people of God. When there is no life, we need to pray that God would breathe on us so that we will awaken and arise in His presence as Adam did.

In reality, the church is not a building. The church is people who have been breathed on and made alive by God based on what Jesus did at the cross. In the New Testament, the Apostle Paul declared to believers that they are now the temple of God where the Holy Spirit lives: *Or do you not know that your body is the temple of the Holy Spirit who is in you, whom you have from God, and you are not your own? For you were bought at a price; therefore glorify God in your body and in your spirit, which are God's* (1 Co 6:19-20). Because you have been bought with a price, the blood of Jesus, you belong to God. You are to glorify God in your body and in your spirit. Let's think of it this way: your body is now the building that a member of the true church lives in. Your body also has become a steeple with a spire on top of it. The spire is up and above its surroundings, indicating a connection with the God of heaven above. This is a picture of what an antenna does in the natural realm. By comparison, you are a living antenna. Inside your body there is a transmitter and a receiver operated by the Holy Spirit. You are able to receive and transmit communication from the unseen world around you. Through the Holy Spirit inside of you, you can communicate with God. Just like a radio or television station does, you can receive information from the unseen realm. Is it not true that the atmosphere around us is filled with all sorts of communications that can be received if you tune in? There are words, pictures, and images zooming around you right now. This is true regardless of where you are on planet Earth. With today's satellite technology, live-as-it-happens news can be heard and seen around the world. These words, pictures, and images are invisible, but they are there just the same. Your receiver determines what you are able to see and hear.

It is important that you have a receiver set to station JESUS. Otherwise you may connect with information that is not coming from Jesus through the Holy Spirit to you. I remember growing up, my Dad got into a CB radio club for awhile. At night, he would sit and talk to other people around the country who tuned into the same frequency. Occasionally, on nights when the weather conditions were just right, we would pick up interference bleeding into the airwaves. This interference was called "skip." Skip is communications from faraway places that literally skip across the bottom of the clouds and are picked up by people listening to their radios. Most people have had times at night when they were scanning the dial on an AM radio and heard people speaking a foreign language from a faraway place. This principle is true in the natural as well. When you play around with the tuner, you may pick up strange voices from strange places. This is the reason it is so important to know the Word of God.

The Bible gives us the parameters of safe operation. By knowing the boundaries that are spelled out in the Bible, we can rest assured that the Lord will always speak to us in a manner that is consistent with what He has already spoken in His written word. When we hear, see, or sense something that is contrary to what the Bible says, we will know it is not the Holy Spirit who is leading us. The Spirit of God will never lead us contrary to the Word of God. He will not contradict Himself, because He was the one who moved upon men and supplied them with the words and truths that have been recorded in the Bible. In the natural, an antenna has a range of receptivity. When you get out of its range, you start getting interference. You hear static in the airwaves. If you get far enough out of bounds, you may pick up a broadcast from another station somewhere and be unaware that you have changed stations. This is how people can become deceived.

The way to guard against deception is to be grounded in the truth. The way to be grounded in the truth is to study the Bible. Please understand that I am not just talking about getting a head full of Bible facts. I am describing allowing the Word of God to get down into your spirit. It must be grafted to your soul, and then it will renew your mind. The way to know if it is really getting inside of you is by the impact it has on your behavior. When fertilizer gets into the roots, it makes its way to the fruit. There have been too many believers who stuff their brains full of biblical information who have never had their lives changed by its truth. The devil can and does quote Scripture. Many atheists can recite passages from the Bible. Quoting and reciting Bible verses is a good thing, but it is not enough to transform our wayward hearts. Knowing and doing the truth results in life change.

Then Jesus said to those Jews who believed Him, "If you abide in My word, you are My disciples indeed. And you shall know the truth, and the truth shall make you free" (Jo 8:31-32). It is abiding or continuing in the truth that results in knowing the truth. Truth brings increasing levels of freedom into our lives. Every antenna needs to be properly grounded in order to work correctly and safely. So, if you are grounded in the Word and learn to listen to the Holy Spirit, He will help you receive information from the unseen realm of heaven, and this will help you to do the will of God here in the earth. We are to pray for "God's will to be done on Earth as it is in heaven." Jesus expects us to be in tune with the world above us so that we impact the world around us. When we learn to tune in and become sensitive to the Holy Spirit, we can start hearing God's voice speaking His words to us. Sometimes, we will receive pictures and images. These can come through dreams, visions, and words of wisdom and knowledge which are gifts of the Holy Spirit. Simply put, the Holy

Spirit may cause a word or picture or knowledge to come into your spirit and invade your mind. When this happens, it is like the Holy Spirit giving a gift to you. He is giving you something that you can give back to God in the form of glory. When you hear from your Heavenly Father and it helps someone, then He is glorified.

Adam was created to hear from God and to see what God wanted him to see. This is the way Jesus lived. He only did what He saw His Father doing and only spoke what He heard His Father speaking. Therefore, He ministered by being in communication with Father. He did this through the Holy Spirit just like we are to do. Like an antenna, we are wired as children of God to transmit and receive in the realm of the spirit. This may seem strange to some people. Isn't prayer the ability to communicate with God? We all believe in prayer. Most of us believe that the Lord will speak to us through His word. Most already believe that they can transmit and receive communication from God. You can become tuned in to hear more and see more than you might think.

This communication from the Holy Spirit has been called by many names. Promptings, leadings, nudges, wooings, premonitions, intuitions, and holy hunches are a few of them. Sometimes they are stronger than other times. Sometimes the Holy Spirit will weave a series of these moments together to create powerful God-inspired experiences in which we participate in the supernatural.

A few Sundays ago, my wife Mikki and I went to a local restaurant after church. Our children were with friends, so we had one of those rare meals alone. While we were waiting to be seated, one of the members of our fellowship came in. He looked at us, and his face lit up. He seemed unusually excited to see us. He proceeded to share with us what he had just experienced. He was on his way out of town when the Holy Spirit placed in his heart to return to this restaurant in town where we would be. He was to pay for our meal. This explained the excitement on his face when he walked in and saw us waiting to be seated. We were also intrigued because we realized that we had chosen to eat at this particular restaurant about three times in three years.

After Mikki and I were seated and eating, the server told us that someone informed her we were very special people and wanted to pay for our meal. In a little bit, she returned and said, "You must be very special people. Someone else wants to pay for your meal as well." I shared with her that I pastored a church in the city and that several of our church members were in the restaurant. As it turned out, the other people who wanted to pay for the meal bought our desserts. During the course of all this, our friend who had driven back to the restaurant by inspiration witnessed to this server and discovered that she was a Christian looking for a church home. When she returned to our table a little later, I heard the gentle voice of the Spirit whispering to me about her. I politely shared with her that I felt the Lord had told me that she was a college student struggling with what direction her education was to take. I sensed that there was some pressure being placed on her to do one thing and her heart was telling her another thing. The Lord wanted her to go with what was in her heart. She confirmed this was her situation. At this point, she wanted to know more about the church we attended. Before we left, we spoke with another server who was a member of our fellowship, and she said she would follow up with her friend. As we left, we marveled at how much the Lord loved this young lady to orchestrate the events as He did. We all were blessed as these moments of inspiration were connected together. It was body ministry at work in the marketplace.

Have you ever had a dream you believed was inspired of God? Most people have. I have had dreams in which God has given me guidance, and I know many other people who have had dreams that helped them to live for God. The Bible has many examples of people who had dreams inspired of God.

Mikki had a dream three months before I was called to serve at Faith Church (formerly called Faith Tabernacle Church). She saw me there behind the pulpit preaching. However, the church building was different than it is now. In the dream, the building was much larger with stadium type seating surrounding the outer walls in a semi-circular pattern. In the dream, there were also people in the audience from the county we were living in at the time, which was over one hour away. None of this added up at the time. The church had spoken to me previously, but I felt I was where God wanted me. I had no intention of moving my family and serving on staff at a church. I was traveling to the nations, preaching at various churches and conferences. We assumed that the dream meant they would build a new worship center, and I would be invited to speak. However, through a chain of events and confirmations, in three months I said yes to the Lord and to Pastor Henry Melton to come to Faith Church. I served 11 months as Pastor Melton's associate until he placed the baton of senior pastor in my hand. I now preach from the pulpit service by service. It has been a wonderful experience for us. We now have people driving from surrounding areas to attend our services, including people from our home county. In addition, we are just finishing phase one of an expansion program and preparing for phase two. Phase two involves the building of a new 3,500-seat worship center with stadium seating. It seems that Mikki's entire dream is coming true. The Holy Spirit showed her a snapshot of things to come.

God does speak to us through dreams, and these are truly inspirational moments. He speaks to us through the Bible. He can speak to us through a friend who is having an inspired moment. He can speak to us through His creation. He speaks through a gentle inner voice. He sometimes speaks through acts of nature. In the Bible, He got a prophet's attention by speaking through a donkey. Peter was convicted by the crowing of a rooster. He will never speak contrary to what He has already said in the Bible, but it is wrong to think that He will not speak to you in other ways. He is a Father, and He loves to listen and talk to His children.

Don't feel inadequate or defeated. If you are a child of God, then His Spirit lives in you. You have what you need to be an inspiration. He can use you to express His thoughts, and at times, you can become His voice to someone in need. Your hands can become His hands to help others. Your feet can become His feet to carry you down the path of God's will for your life. Your eyes can see what His eyes are seeing, and your ears can hear what His voice is speaking. George Washington Carver, the great agriculturist and inventor, said, "I love to think of nature as an unlimited broadcasting station, through which God speaks to us every hour, if we will only tune in." You can be a broadcasting station, an inspiration station in your home, office, classroom, and marketplace, even to the ends of the earth. Stay tuned in and who knows what could happen! In his book, *The Greatest Thing in the World*, Henry Drummon stated, "The greatest thing a man can do for his Heavenly Father is to be kind to some of his other children." Don't overcomplicate what I have shared in this chapter. Simply ask Father God to help you help others—then listen. Make the choice to be usable. Raise your antenna. Open your hands and stretch them toward heaven and ask God to use you. He will. If you furnish the cable, God will furnish the power!

A quote I once read reminds us that we should, "Aspire to inspire before we expire." When you get Jesus, you get inspired! The same Holy Spirit that breathed on God's Word to make it alive will breathe on you to bring life to what you do. Learn to tune in to the frequency which you were created to hear. Let your life be an antenna pointing toward God. Let Jesus use your life to be an inspiration to the world around you. The inspirational life is not bound by the natural; it is supernatural. Read on!

SEVENTEEN

THE SUPERNATURAL ADAM

God is and all is well.

John Whittier

In this age of callousness, we need the power of God operating in our lives. The power of God was never intended to be reduced to a doctrine that would cause division among God's people; it was intended to change people's lives. Too many arguments have resulted in a lot of *dialogue* about the power of God but with no *display* of that power. Many have no difficulty in ascribing power to Satan, who is wreaking havoc on so many lives, yet they are hesitant to encourage believers to rely on the power of the Holy Spirit in their lives. This thinking is inconsistent at best and dangerous at worst. I certainly do not have all the answers that people ask concerning the operation of God's power in today's world, but I do encourage people that it is always right to simply believe that *with God all things are possible* (Mk 10:27). The same God who split the sea, shut the lion's mouth, buckled Goliath's knees, and tumbled Jericho's walls is still alive and well today. He is not in a supernatural drought. He is **GOD!** He has the power to blast the hard shells off the hearts of men and women who have lived their lives without Him. He has the power to do the impossible and enjoys the glory He receives when He does. He has the power to help you in your most desperate situation. He is not without the means to release miracles into your life. We need His power working in and through our lives!

Adam's first moment of existence was a supernatural experience. Adam was naturally supernatural. He knew nothing but living in the supernatural. To him, there was no distinguishing between the two. He was created through a supernatural power to live a supernatural life. He walked and talked with God as best friends do. When the breath of God was breathed on the dust that would become Adam, it was an awesome supernatural display of creative power. Adam was the result of supernatural activity, created to live and experience the supernatural. God's intentions for man have not changed. He still *invites* us to experience a supernatural life. Adam was a miracle man! You too were created to live in the realm of the miraculous. I have learned that this same supernatural, miraculous breath that breathed on Adam is still breathing supernaturally and miraculously on people today. I have seen it with my eyes and have felt it in my soul. Because of this, I now have a passion to see God's purposes fulfilled in my life and the lives of other people.

Passion and purpose are two buzzwords in the kingdom these days, and they should be. Being motivated by a burning love to see God's purposes fulfilled in our lives should not be considered strange; it should be the norm. We were not destined to live life in the basement hidden away from the light and life of God. We were made to walk the earth as children of Almighty God. Our spiritual DNA links us with Jesus Christ Himself. Jesus came to do what He was sent to do. He had purpose. So do you and I. We must get in sync with that purpose and allow the wind of God to carry us where He wills. When He breathes on a lifeless marriage and it comes alive, it is awesome to behold. When He breathes on a prodigal and he starts running home, it is truly spectacular! When He breathes on a disease-ridden body and it regains strength, it is a remarkable sight.

One Sunday evening at our church in Florence, Alabama, the breath of God was breathed on a young woman and we witnessed a true miracle of God. Our ushers saw a car pull up into the drive-through area by the entrance doors. They noticed something unusual was taking place in the car. As they approached, they witnessed a young woman crying in pain as she sat in the front passenger's seat. In the car with her were her father and mother. They had just brought their daughter, Kim, from Eliza Coffee Memorial Hospital. In fact,

Kim was transported from the hospital to her parents' house by ambulance. Upon arrival at their house, they simply loaded Kim into their car and headed toward the church. It is important to understand what had precipitated their arrival at the church.

Earlier in the week, Kim had gone to the hospital. She was admitted and placed in the Intensive Care Unit. She was having extreme pain in her body. She would lose her sight and become nonresponsive. Her respiratory system was shutting down. Her condition became so critical that when they had her sign a living will, her hand was held by a nurse while she made a mark that indicated her signature. She was unable to sign her name. Family members, friends, and the people with whom she worked came by the ICU to say their good-byes. She approached death but then stabilized enough to be put in a regular room. The doctors were not able to diagnose what was happening and were unable to do anything more for her. They sent her home on Sunday to be cared for by home heath care while they worked to get her a place at Vanderbilt Hospital in Nashville, Tennessee.

Kim's parents testified that they heard the Lord speak to them to take Kim to church. They agreed that they would somehow carry her to the church to receive prayer. Please understand this was a family who did not attend our church. They knew of Faith and knew some of our members. Faith is a nondenominational church made up of people from about every denominational background you can imagine. We have a good relationship with other churches in the city, and we all work together for the kingdom. Kim and her family were members of a precious Baptist congregation in town. I could relate to them because I pastored in Southern Baptist churches for almost 15 years prior to pastoring Faith Church.

When Kim and her parents arrived at the church, Kim was still wearing her hospital gown and bracelet. The ushers brought a wheelchair out to the car to help her into the church. She was screaming in pain. She would ride a few feet in the chair, but the pain was too unbearable. They would hold her under her arms and let her take a few steps, but the pain was unbearable. She continued to cry and scream. It took them several minutes to move her about 75 feet down the foyer area to the prayer room. They continued alternating back and forth in and out of the chair until they were able to lay her on a couch in the prayer room.

Kim and her parents had arrived at the church at about 5:00 p.m.

At the time of their arrival, I was overseeing a new members' reception. Many of our staff and leaders were at the reception. Brother Henry and several of our prayer warriors began praying with Kim. Dan Blessing, who is now our executive administrator, informed me that there was a lady in the prayer room who needed attention. I told him I had to honor the commitment at the reception and that I would come as soon as I could. Mikki went on to the prayer room to help. I was sent for one more time, and I repeated my answer to them. Finally, at 5:50 p.m., I made my way to the prayer room. When I walked in, I immediately came under conviction when I saw the pain this young woman was enduring. I should have been more sensitive to the Holy Spirit. There were several people in the room praying for Kim as she agonized in pain. I kneeled down beside her. There were tears streaming out of her eyes. She was writhing in pain. I began to join others in praying for her healing. Then…the breath of God came.

All at once, as the Holy Spirit helped me, I knew some things that I did not know before. I saw a place under a set of stairs. I also sensed something was very wrong. It was a feeling of darkness and oppression. I sensed that witchcraft was at work against this family. When I shared this with Kim, she cried more loudly, telling me what it meant. It was something very specific to her circumstances. She and her husband, Del, had been separated. He was sleeping under the stairs at his parents' house. I led Kim through a simple prayer repenting and renouncing bitterness and the work of witchcraft against them. I looked at her and prayed, "Be loosed and be healed in Jesus' name!"

She stopped crying.

In a moment, she sat up and placed her feet on the floor without pain. In another minute or so, she said she wanted to stand up. We helped her stand up. Then she wanted to walk on her own. We stepped back, and she began to take some little steps. We were all astonished. Her hands shot up in the air, and she began to praise God and to cry again. This time it was not the cry of pain, but the cry of joy. Through her tears, she said, "I'm going to be able to see my little boy grow up." Zac was her seven-year-old son. We were all in awe at what God had instantaneously done, and we all knew it was God who did it. The sweet Holy Spirit had brought the breath and life of God upon her through the name of Jesus. He did in a moment what no man had been able to do for her at all. To be honest, though we had asked God to touch Kim, we were all stunned when He did. It was such a remarkable thing to witness. All of us knew that God had chosen to visit and release His power upon her life.

The evening service had already started, so we rejoiced with them for a few moments, telling them to let us know if there was any other way we could help. We made our way into the service, and they made their way to the parking lot. When I got up to preach about 45 minutes later, I was surprised to see Kim and her family on the back row in the sanctuary. She still had on her hospital gown. When they got into the car to go home, they decided that they could not leave. They wanted to stay for the service, so they returned. What a joy!

A couple of weeks later as I was ministering at the conclusion of the service, a young woman in her thirties approached me with a big smile on her face. I looked at her, and she just smiled. She could tell I did not know who she was. She said, "I'm Kim." I did not recognize her. She was dressed in her Sunday best, her hair was in place, and her face shone with joy. What a powerful transformation had taken place. Kim informed me she was doing wonderfully well. There were people who later told her mother that they were sorry they were unable to attend Kim's funeral. They had assumed Kim had died. They were shocked to learn that she had recovered. Within a few months, God did a mighty work, and Del and Kim were reconciled and remarried. They, along, with their son, Zac, are very faithful members of our congregation. They are now involved in ministries in the church. In fact, as I sit here writing about them, they are in Orlando at Disney World, riding the rides on a family vacation. Every time I see Kim, I think of how awesome God is.

This is just one example I have witnessed in the past few years of what happens when God supernaturally breathes on a person or a situation. I certainly do not claim to know how it all works. I just know there are times when God breathes and reminds us that He is God. Seeing God move in this way reminds us that He is God, and we are not! This is the part of the adventure of understanding the breath of God. You and I, like Adam, were made to live with the presence of God touching our lives. Don't settle for a life void of the supernatural. To do so is to settle for a life where God is not seen as a reality but as a fantasy.

Knowing what God wanted when He made Adam will help us

know what He wanted when He made you. If He can breathe on dust and make a man, then He can breathe on a man and make a miracle. He can breathe on you, and you can see miracles. I like what G. K. Chesterton once said: "The most wonderful thing about miracles is that they sometimes happen." It sure is fun when they do. At the same time, it is powerfully sobering to see the majesty of God in such a way. This great God of miracles is our Heavenly Father, who enjoys hanging out with us and wants to do miraculous things through us. Let's not argue about whether or not miracles can happen, let's just pray that they will. In the next chapter, I want to challenge you to learn to recognize where God is working. When God breathes on something, there are evidences that it is Him.

EIGHTEEN

THE BREATH OF LIFE

I cannot explain the wind, but I can hoist a sail!

Anonymous

Has your mind ever been invaded by the thought of another person, and you later learned that there was an urgent need occurring in that person's life at the precise time they were on your mind? Have you ever awakened in the middle of the night with a desire to read a particular Bible verse, and then later that day the verse became a source of direction for you in a specific situation? Have you ever felt a tug to share the message of God's love with a stranger and when you did they gave their heart to Jesus? These occasions were times when the breath of God was breathed on you.

Life becomes a great adventure when we learn to watch and wait for the breath of God to be breathed on us. This is the way man was intended to live his life. Until God breathed on Adam, he was just dust. Adam's life began by the breath of God being breathed on him, and our lives are sustained by the breath of God being breathed on us. In the previous two chapters, I wrote about the inspired life and the supernatural life. In this chapter, I want to encourage you to learn to recognize when the breath of God is being breathed on you.

The words *death* and *breath* sound very similar, but there is quite a difference in the meanings of the two words. Where there's breath there is no death. Where there is death, there is no breath. However, it seems that there remains some confusion between the two words in some places and among some people. The breath of God is the breath of life. Since God is life and He gives breath to all creation, then His breath is the breath of life. As Genesis 2:7 indicates, it was the breath of life breathed on dust that brought Adam into existence. (*And the* LORD *God formed man of the dust of the ground, and breathed into his nostrils the breath of life; and man became a living being* (Ge 2:7).)

What a powerful force the breath of life is! Where God breathes, there is the release of the breath of life. There is a quickening and awakening that begins to occur. This simple truth, if applied to our daily walk with God, could do a lot to increase our level of discernment. How often has the church been guilty of trying to keep something alive that God is not breathing on? I have adopted into my terminology the phrase "breath of God" to help me in discerning what God is blessing and what God is not blessing. If God is breathing on something, it will demonstrate the signs of life. If He is not, it will require a lot of human effort to make it look alive. He has not called us to be morticians who learn how to make the dead look alive. We must learn "Where there is no breath there is death." Paramedics who arrive at the scene of an accident and find an unconscious victim quickly look for signs of life. The world is looking at the church and looking for the same thing. The world is checking the vital signs of today's church and wondering if there is a pulse. A.W. Tozer said it well: "One hundred religious persons knit into a unity by careful organization do not constitute a church any more than eleven dead men make a football team. The first requisite is life, always." We should pray for our churches, ministries, and lives to be fruitful and full of the life of God. Charles Haddon Spurgeon said, "A church in the land without the Spirit is rather a curse than a blessing. If you have not the Spirit of God, Christian worker, remember that you stand in somebody else's way; you are a fruitless tree standing where a fruitful tree might grow." I agree with Spurgeon.

The question "Is God breathing on this?" will save all of us needless energy and pain. Too often we have deceived ourselves into celebrating a corpse. We decorate our programs. We dress up our plans. We talk of the corpse as though it were alive. We hear the reading of the obituary of our sacred cows and accuse people of being too radical and judgmental. Sometimes a big *cook-out* featuring our sacred cows might provide the fire we need for revival. Keeping pulse-less programs on life support is exhausting and expensive. We refuse to hold a funeral thinking if we will just keep holding on, it will somehow become what we want it to be. This kind of thinking is the problem. It is not about what *we* want it to be; it is about what God wants it to be. I once heard a phrase that sums it up: "When the horse dies, dismount!" How silly for the *world* to look at the *church* and ask the question, "Why are those people still sitting on the dead horse?" We need a new staff position in our churches called *Spiritual Coroner* whose responsibility it is to give the official word that something is dead. I have drawn the conclusion that the Lord wants us to learn how to pronounce some things *dead*. At least then we will know we need resurrection power to make the dead live again. If the seed of God is in something, it will rise again. Burial precedes resurrection. Even in our own lives, we have to die before we can truly live.

Let me use a simple illustration to help you discern the breath of God. A sailboat is made to be carried by the wind. When the wind is blowing and the sails are hoisted, the boat is moving. When the wind is blowing and the sails are not hoisted, the movement of the boat is minimized. When the sails are hoisted and the wind is not blowing, it's a pretty and peaceful sight, but the boat is not going anywhere. In order to move the boat when the wind is not blowing, an alternative source of power must be employed. In such a case, you will have to row or rely upon a man-made machine to move the boat. In our churches, we have all become adept at using alternative sources of power. We rev up our man-made machines, and the boat begins to move. From a distance, it looks as if it is being carried by the wind, but it is not. It has to have fuel added to it constantly. It has to have continual maintenance. It requires a lot more human attention and work to keep it going. There are times when we pull in our sails because we feel they slow the boat down. We become addicted and fully rely on the man-made motor to carry us where we want to go. The thing we really like about the man-made motor is we get to control when it starts and stops and how fast it goes.

At other times, we do not look to the machine; we simply pull up our shirt sleeves and start rowing. Rather than waiting on the wind, we row. The movement excites us for awhile, but then we become tired, frustrated, and disillusioned. We find ourselves singing a new hymn in our services.

Row, row, row your boat
Gently up the stream.
Wearily, wearily, wearily, wearily,
No life—it's just a dream.

Because of this, many people no longer want to ride the boat. It's too much work. The rowers become worn out, restless, and grumpy. They ignorantly point to the sails and ask, "What are those things for?"

We need the wind of God to blow into our lives and our churches. Only the breath of God can carry us where God wants us to go. Only the breath of the life of God can cause the corpse to live. When Jesus walked the earth, He regularly broke up funerals!

God can bring the dead to life. It happens every Sunday morning in many churches when the benediction is prayed. At the final "Amen!" the dead arise and race to the restaurants. Seriously, He *can* make the dead live. This is the heart of the teaching on the resurrection. He can revive the dying congregation and bring it back to life. He can restore feeling to the numbed zombies who robotically keep going and going though they do not know where. He can revive the marriage where love has taken a vacation. He can bring back life to the prodigal who has fled away from home chasing a dream built out of cotton candy. He can make dry bones live.

In the book of Ezekiel, the prophet had a vision of a valley of dry bones. God used the vision to encourage Ezekiel that though the nation of Israel looked as though she would never live again, she could and she would. Ezekiel was able to see into the future when God would do a glorious restoration of the nation of Israel.

The hand of the LORD came upon me and brought me out in the Spirit of the LORD, and set me down in the midst of the valley; and it was full of bones. Then He caused me to pass by them all around, and behold, there were very many in the open valley; and indeed they were very dry. And He said to me, "Son of man, can these bones live? So I answered, "O Lord God, You know." Again He said to me, "Prophesy to these bones, and say to them, 'O dry bones, hear the word of the LORD! Thus says the Lord God to these bones: "Surely I will cause breath to enter into you, and you shall live.

Ezekiel 37:1-5

You may feel like you live in Drybonesville. Dry bones mean the funeral is over, the flowers have dried, and the tombstone is in place. Dry bones mean only memories of the past remain. Dry bones mean the celebration has turned into a cemetery. If there had been a church in Ezekiel's vision, it probably would have been called, Dead Bones Valley Church. The church motto would have been "Ruts are Underrated." It would have been pastored by Dr. Rigor Mortis. The pastor's favorite sermon would have been "Dust Thou Art and to Dust Thou Shalt Return." The congregation's favorite hymns would have been "Just As I Was," "Precious Memories," and "He Lived." It is important to call something what it *is* before you call it what it can *become*. Ezekiel called it dry bones. Then by obeying God he could begin to call it what it was going to become. This is how faith operates. E. M. Bounds, a man of God known for his passion to see a praying church revival, said, "What the Church needs today is not more machinery or better, not new organizations or more and novel methods, but men whom the Holy Ghost can use—men of prayer, men mighty in prayer. The Holy Ghost does not flow through methods, but through men. He does not come on machinery, but on men. He does not anoint plans, but men, men of prayer."

This is really what we are praying for when we pray for revival. *Revive* means "to relive." To see things live again the way they once lived is what revival is about. When revival comes, things are brought back into order and the life of God is flowing as it is supposed to. What is it that causes things to live again? It is the breath of God. The Lord told Ezekiel to prophesy to the bones. However, it was the breath that brought life into the bones.

So I prophesied as I was commanded; and as I prophesied, there was a noise, and suddenly a rattling; and the bones came together, bone to bone. Indeed, as I looked, the sinews and the flesh came upon them, and the skin covered them over; but there was *no breath in them. Also He said to me, "Prophesy to the breath, prophesy, son of man, and say to the breath, 'Thus says the Lord GOD: "Come from the four winds, O breath, and breathe on these slain, that they may live."'" So I prophesied as He commanded me, and breath came into them, and they lived, and stood upon their feet, an exceedingly great army.*

Ezekiel 37:7-10

Yes, if God tells us, we can speak life over something that is dead and it can live. Too often we start prophesying without the Lord telling us to prophesy. This is presumption and a waste of time. But when God leads us to express our faith and prophesy to a situation that seems hopeless, we will see Him send the wind and turn things around. He will always honor His own word. His word and His wind hang out together.

When God's breath of life is breathed, dust becomes a man. When the breath of God leaves, the man becomes dust again. Adam's body was dust before it became the travel unit for Adam's spirit. It was the spirit life of God in Adam that enabled him to live and move and have his being. The Spirit produces movement. It is the same with the church on Earth today. It is God's Spirit that enables the church to move. Anything else is man-made and robotic at best and demonic at worst.

I agree that Adam was created to become a *living being* not a *living doing*. We have substituted the identity of our being with our doing. God created us to be. Our doing should flow out of our being. When you make the mistake of thinking that your being flows out of your doing, you are setting yourself up for one enormous misery session. We must understand that we are mere vessels (boats) made by God. Creating the wind is God's job. We can hoist our sails, but we cannot manufacture the wind. We, as the early church did, must learn to wait on the wind before we rush out to change the world. Setting off under the power of the oar or the machine may get us moving, but it may carry us to the wrong destination. How sad that we could actually find ourselves harbored in a place not marked on God's plan for our lives. Better to hoist our sails and let the wind do the work. This is the sound that birthed the early church. The sound of heaven's wind filled the place where they prayed, and they went out under the power of the Holy Spirit. The result was thousands saved and miracles abounding. Jesus taught Nicodemus that the way a person experiences the new birth is through the unseen mysterious work of the Spirit of God. Just as God breathed on Adam and brought him to life, He still breathes on lost souls and brings them to life.

A moment when the wind comes can do more than years of rowing and fueling our man-made motors. The breath of God turns dry bones into living armies. The great awakenings that have stirred our nation and other nations in days gone by are proof of what happens when heaven's wind comes. Where God breathes, there is life. Our substitutes have proven ineffective in sparing souls, saving marriages, and reviving churches. We may fabricate things that resemble the breath of life, but the proof is in what is produced by what is released. Today's church has become adept at stirring emotions but stopping short of transformation. At other times, we rob people of their emotions, and they feel trapped with no way to express the longings of their hearts. We must let the wind blow where it wills. This may mean opening a few windows we have shut for fear of a breeze disrupting our neatly arranged programs. It may mean allowing the doors to be swung open wide so the wind can cleanse our churches of the dust that has been accumulating for too long. Who knows? God may take some of that dust and make something new and alive out of it. He's done it before, He can do it again.

There is a story attributed to the great missionary, Hudson Taylor, whom God used to greatly impact China in a previous generation. When Hudson Taylor went to China, he made the voyage on a boat. As it neared the channel between the southern Malay Peninsula and the island of Sumatra, the missionary heard an urgent knock on his stateroom door. He opened it, and there stood the captain of the ship. "Mr. Taylor," he said, "we have no wind. We are drifting toward an island where the people are heathen, and I fear they are cannibals."

"What can I do?" asked Taylor.

"I understand that you believe in God. I want you to pray for wind."

"All right, Captain, I will, but you must set the sail."

"Why, that's ridiculous! There's not even the slightest breeze. Besides, the sailors will think I'm crazy." But finally, because of Taylor's insistence, he agreed. Forty-five minutes later, he returned and found the missionary still on his knees. "You can stop praying now," said the captain. "We've got more wind than we know what to do with!"[15] This story encourages us to pray. Hudson Taylor prayed and the wind came. The early church was praying when the wind came. I'm waiting for such a reply from the world in response to the prayers of the church of today, "Stop praying! We have more wind than we know what to do with!"

And suddenly there came a sound from heaven, as of a rushing mighty wind, and it filled the whole house where they were sitting (Ac 2:2). The very act of praying and crying out to God is an indication that we do not have what it takes to do what needs to be done. This dependence of our heart upon the heart of God will bring the wind from heaven. Helplessness is a virtue in the kingdom. We must possess hearts that confess, "If God does not move, we will not move." It is the pure heart that wants to see God. It is the heart that is tired of explaining things in the natural and is hungry for the unexplainable of the supernatural to occur. People are yearning to see and hear that which can only be understood as a work of God in their midst. The substitutes have lost their flavor, and the imitations no longer have the appeal they once possessed.

Dear Reader, there is a hurting world around you, and God wants to use you to change it. He wants to breathe on you! Yes, *you!* Don't look over your shoulder for someone else to volunteer. The Lord wants to breathe on you in a fresh and dynamic way. When He does, you will be changed and you will become an agent of change in this world. This is the promise of Jesus to those who would follow and pursue Him to the ends of the earth.

But you shall receive power when the Holy Spirit has come upon you; and you shall be witnesses to Me in Jerusalem, and in all Judea and Samaria, and to the end of the earth (Ac 1:8). Notice it is "you" who will receive power to become an agent of change. His breath breathed on you will awaken boldness within you to bear witness of Jesus Christ. He can use your breath to share with people beginning from where you are right now to the very ends of the earth. There are no limitations to His using you. You can be one who prophesies to the wind. You can see dry bones converted into soldiers.

As the dry bones in Ezekiel's vision needed the breath of God to blow upon them in order to live, there are many people who need it as well. Who needs the breath of God? The lonely, grieving parent going through the agony of moving furniture out of the apartment that their college-aged daughter occupied before the tragic accident. The broken-hearted divorcee struggling under the weight of the guilt and pain of a failed marriage. The single mom looking for a decent way to provide for the three children she has to raise alone. The heart surgeon scrubbing his hands before stepping into an operating room where a man's life hangs in the balance. The policeman who has just pulled over a suspicious vehicle and feels his heart racing as adrenaline pumps into his system. The man walking out of an office complex holding the personal belongings that had filled his desk until a pink slip was placed in his hand. The couple holding hands in the ICU waiting room at the children's hospital. The pastor slumped over his desk in depression because he has trouble finding the God he regularly recommends to others. The housewife who feels worthless and trapped because she has what she thought she had always wanted. In short, anyone in need of hope is a prime candidate for the breath of God, and anyone willing to be used can be used to deliver that hope. The Lord has and still does turn hopeless ash heaps into monuments of His grace. This is when He gets His greatest glory!

Your failures, excuses, and reasons for being unusable will crumble under the weight and power of His breath breathed on you. We all have areas of our lives that need improvement. Even Adam had a lot of *dirt* in his life before God breathed on him! Seriously, I know we all realize when He breathed on Adam, He breathed on a perfect creation. Yet, there are many instances when He breathed on men whose heads had hung in defeat and failure and women who carried the stain of guilt on their lives. God uses imperfect people to help imperfect people. Knowing that God breathes on imperfect people also gives hope to broken hearts. If He breathed on Moses, who killed a man, and David, who committed adultery, it gives us hope that He will breathe on us.

The only people who the Father has available to work through down here are imperfect people. The perfect congregation with a perfect pastor does not exist. The perfect marriage with the perfect couple does not exist. The perfect parent with the perfect children cannot be found here on the earth. But imperfect congregations, pastors, marriages, parents, and children all serve a perfect God who in His perfection always knows just what we need in every situation. His perfection enables us to be usable because He makes available to us through His grace and mercy what we need in our time of need. Whether it is dry bones, a pile of dust, or the situation you are in, the breath of God can revive and restore. Right now, while your faith is being stirred, make an altar out of this moment, hoist your sails and pray for wind!

FATHER'S HOME
FOR YOU

Nineteen

With God in the Garden

All that God requires of us is an opportunity to show what He can do.
A.B. Simpson

The LORD God planted a garden eastward in Eden, and there He put the man whom He had formed.

Genesis 2:8

In our DNA, there is a distant memory of the love and pleasure of living in the Garden of Eden (Pleasure). God planted a garden, and then He planted a man in the garden. Adam lived in a garden. Men still love the great outdoors. I believe one reason that people want to spend time in nature is that they are lonely for God and don't know it. Adam and Eve were made to live in a garden and enjoy God's presence. Jesus often drew away to a garden to spend time with His Heavenly Father. Eden's garden was the center of activity between God and man until the fall. Since the dawn of time, man has enjoyed the thrill of feeling one with nature. Most families take vacation time and head for some place where natural scenic beauty abounds. It may be the sugar white sands of the Gulf coast, the snow-capped peaks of the Rockies, the fog-draped mountains of the Smoky Mountains, the expansive gorges of the Grand Canyon, the towering redwoods of Northern California, or the multi-faceted beauties of Yellowstone. The human heart is moved by the scenes, smells, and silence of nature.

Being able to experience time away in nature brings us back to our most primitive roots. I believe when we purposely draw away into nature to meet with God, great things can happen. It just feels right. After all, it's where our oldest ancestor had his start. Memories of emotional past events are powerful to us all. Revisiting places where your life was touched can touch you again. Standing at the gravesite of a loved one can stir feelings deep inside of you. Going back to the school where you graduated for a reunion can put some kick in your quest for nostalgia. The altar where you kissed your spouse after the "I do" can cause the memory bubbles to begin bursting. It is this kind of feeling that fills the heart when you see the ocean, a redwood, the Rockies, or the Grand Canyon. Something is awakened and stirred in your soul. It could be that quiet is often present in these places that cannot be found in our normal, daily lives. It could be the breath-taking beauty of these sights that remind us someone out there had to make all of this by design. It could be the connection with the primitive part of our ancestral roots. It could be the distant memory of Eden deep inside of us. It is probably a combination of it all.

A friend of mine once told me of an experience he had when he was away from home on a business trip. In another state, he was overcome by a feeling of loneliness and longing. He missed his family. He changed his plans and spent hours making the long drive home to be with his wife and children. Upon his arrival home, he greeted his wife and children and spent time with them. He realized that the same sense of loneliness was still strong and alive inside of him. He then proceeded to his bedroom, closed the door, and got on his knees before God. It was then he realized that his heart had been longing for God. We all have this longing for God. How many times have we tried to fill the longing with something other than God?

When we spend a day in the woods or a week's vacation in nature, we get a little closer to that place where we all started. It makes us feel good. It makes us review what's important. However, when we go back home without meeting with God, we fall short of the splendor that could have been a part of the trip.

I imagine that God's heart was thrilled at seeing what He made. He Himself called it good and very good! He liked what He had created for His children. It was certainly a place of stunning scenic beauty. We know how beautiful certain places still are; can you imagine the beauty of the Garden of Eden? A sparkling river bubbling and teaming with life flowed through paradise. Flowers, trees, and exotic plants in all sorts of colors displayed a great variety of fashion which clothed the garden with pristine wonder. Imagine the fragrance of that special place. A thousand peach orchards ripened with sweet fruit could not have matched the smell that must have wafted on the breezes of Eden's mornings. Weedless flower beds! Now that's a novel thought, but that was Eden. It was quite a wedding gift to be placed into the hands of two newlyweds.

I can only imagine what it must have been like to wake up each morning in Eden's Garden. Hearing the birds chirping their morning songs and seeing the sun paint her multicolored streaks across the horizon of a new day while being surrounded by a canopy of green must have been exhilarating. Who would need caffeine if you could awaken in a place like Eden? Let's have fun for a moment! Imagine with me. Upon arising from my place of seamless sleep, I simply walk through a beautiful buffet of bowing limbs that contain all kinds of luscious fruits offering me my first meal of the day. For an early morning stroll, I walk through the garden on safari, seeing the many beautiful creatures that God has created with the knowledge that none of them would dare try to harm me. This was Adam's house and was beyond anything we could imagine. It must have been quite "the place." Yes, Adam and Eve really had it made. Literally, they had it made *for* them.

What an awesome builder, artist, and engineer God is! He built the universe, filled it with all kinds of variety, and it works harmoniously with God's intentions—with the exception of our human family. While everything else in the universe pretty much does what it is *supposed* to do, man seems bent on doing what he *wants* to do. At least, this has been the major issue in my own life. My acute observation skills also inform me that some of the rest of you struggle with this as well! Think of the sweet deal Adam and Eve walked away from when they listened to the serpent. They left the place of rest and ended up in the place of restlessness. All of us have spent time in the place called restlessness.

In the spring of 1983, the Lord began to deal with me about what I was to do with my life. I had been working on a construction crew for a couple of years, and I was becoming restless. I have learned that when we are restless, change is coming. In such times, I ask the Lord if there is anything out of order in my life. I get restless if I lose my peace. There is no rest without the peace of God in my heart. If that is not the issue, then I know the Lord is about to shift something in my life. Like the mother eagle who removes the fluff from the nest so the little eaglets will be encouraged to fly, the Lord often allows us to become uncomfortable so we will move on with Him. On a Sunday night in April after the service had concluded, I went back into the church building and knelt at the altar. I was tired of being miserable and uncomfortable. Things were out of order in my life and needed to shift and change. It was that night I submitted to the Lord. Though I had known the Lord from the age of ten, I had not fully understood or surrendered to His plan for my life. That night I did. I prayed, "Lord, I'll do whatever you tell me to do. I'll go wherever you tell me to go. I'll say whatever you tell me to say." Before I stood up from the altar, I knew I was supposed to preach the gospel. It is hard to describe how I knew this, but I did. The Lord just put it so strong inside of me, I could not deny it. I said, "Yes!" to God's plan for my life. However, I had no idea how much change would come my way *because* I said, "Yes!"

Immediately after this act of consecration and surrender, I was filled with a hunger to study the Bible. I had never experienced this degree of hunger to study anything. I fell in love with the Word of God. I became so fascinated with its stories and truths.

Like Adam and Eve hung out with God in the garden, I started spending a lot of time in the woods with God. Mikki and I had built a house on five wooded acres that were situated in the middle of a much larger spread belonging to her dad. Our gravel driveway was one-quarter mile long. If we ever heard a car, we knew someone was lost or we had company. Being raised in the country, we were both at home there. Almost daily, I would grab my Bible and walk down into the canopy of trees to pray and preach. I would preach to the hardwoods. I suppose this was my preparation for preaching to the *hardheads* later on. Seriously, there were times I would preach at the top of my voice. I would imagine people sitting and listening to my message. I have often stated that if trees could be saved, we had a sanctified forest in our backyard. The oaks and pines would stand and listen to me *preach*. I would read my Bible. I would pray. I would proclaim the Word of God. As the wind blew, they would bow their limbs and wag their leaves at me. The clouds overhead would pan the sky as I looked toward heaven and prayed. It was always so peaceful there. I didn't get many "Amens" other than the occasional squawk of a wood hen or the chatter of a gray squirrel. However, I did get a lot of affirmation from my Heavenly Father. It just felt right because I was stepping into my destiny. It had taken me a while to discover it, but when it happened, it felt so right.

On June 12, 1983, I preached my first sermon. I had studied hours and hours and hours. I was so nervous. I preached about everything I knew that morning, and fifteen minutes later I was finished. That was the beginning of my public ministry. I must admit, a fifteen-minute sermon is no longer a strain. Cutting it down to 40 minutes is the strain.

I think our destiny is similar to Adam's relationship to the Garden of Eden. He knew he was in the right place at the right time, and it brought peace and joy to him. This is how I felt. It was as if the tumblers fell into place, the lock disengaged, and the door of destiny had been opened to me. I would later discover that destiny is not a one-time experience. It is a lifelong journey. Since 1983, there have been many other times that restlessness came, I was changed, and my life shifted into new experiences.

I have noticed a correlation between my getting away in a place of solitude and my being able to hear from God. How many times have we set ourselves up for major heartache because we make major decisions on impulse? We have become so accustomed in our culture to doing things on the run that we have forgotten about "walking" with God in the garden in the cool of the day. One morning recently, while waiting at a red light, I looked into my rearview mirror. I became instantly entertained by what I saw. This precious "on the move" lady was talking on a cell phone held in her left hand. In her right hand, she held the mascara wand she was using to paint her eyelashes. Of course to do this, she had to stare into the rearview mirror which had been tilted toward her face. When the light changed, I took off and did what I was not supposed to do. I drove through the intersection with my eyes darting back and forth from the road in front of me to the lady behind me. As I suspected, she raced along with her cell phone crunched between the left side of her head and the top of her left shoulder. This freed her left hand to steer, at least part of the time. The rest of the time, she used it to adjust the phone that kept slipping off her ear. I assume that when her hand was off the steering wheel she used her knee to steady it and hold the car in the road. I could see her mouth moving as she continued her obviously important conversation. In addition, she allowed her eyes to dart back and forth between a glimpse of my bumper and her eyelashes, which she continued to paint with her right hand. Of course, she had no clue what was going on behind her because her rearview mirror had been adjusted from the rear of her car to the view of her face! She couldn't use her side mirrors because that would have meant dropping her cell phone or making a black slash across her cheeks with her mascara wand. Yet, she was able to do this. She eventually zoomed on around me, charging off into the day, perhaps late for work. By the time she moved around me, she was working on her lips with a tube of lipstick. As her bumper disappeared around the curve before me, I was a little disappointed. I really wanted to see how she was going to drink a sip of her coffee, which I imagined to be waiting in her cup holder releasing its enchanting and enticing aroma into her car. It's understood that women can out-multi-task men any day of the week, but this dear lady was a moving marvel and a state trooper's nightmare all at the same time.

She had a lot of options she could have chosen. She could have told the person on the phone that she would call them back later. She could have waited till she got to the parking lot at work to do her make-up. However, this would have probably meant being late. Being pretty is usually chosen over being tardy by most, but if being pretty and on time for work is possible, most people will juggle dangerously to pull it off. She could have been talking on the phone going over things at work with someone because she was already late. This means that she should have left her house earlier, but then again, I did not hear the kids crying, the husband asking where his socks were, the cat scratching at the back door wanting food while the dog barked at the microwave, reminding her that presto breakfast was ready and waiting. All of this may have happened before she got into her car and saw she had a run in her hose, which sent her back into the land of mayhem once again. This snapshot I got of her at the red light may have been a reflection of what her life is like every day. By the way, was that lady you or your wife, by chance?

This story, while comical, is also typical of many or our lives. We've all read the bumper sticker that says, "I owe, I owe, so off to work I go." We often feel like little yellow pellets being gobbled up by the insatiable Pac-Man called "hurry." The family kitchen is used less and less, and our mini-vans have become meals-on-wheels. We operate in a drive-through culture, having learned how to live life on the fly. It really is a bit crazy when we push the pause button to breathe and consider what we are doing to ourselves. Pulling our hair out in distress only helps the hair implant industry. Yelling at each other doesn't help. We can't slow down out of fear we will get rear-ended by the lady behind us who is painting her eyelashes. Our attention spans have shrunk to the point we can't even remember a train of thought. I am not exempt from the insanity of it all either. This spring, I signed a one-year contract for a company to mow my lawn on the same day I purchased a membership at a local gym so I could exercise. My lawn is mowed while my membership card continues to hide in my wallet. Doesn't make sense, does it? The American lifestyle is good for *business* because it is so filled with *busyness*. What is my point? I am challenging you to get away occasionally and drink in some fresh air, smell the fragrances of the wild, hear the sounds of nature, and quiet your soul before God. I have never had a man on his deathbed tell me he should have spent more time at work. I have had many share they should have spent more time with family and with God.

Adam's first memory was of a life alone with God in the midst of the big woods. Eve's first memory was of a life alone with God in the midst of a beautiful garden. After each had been alone with God, then they were able to come together to fulfill their commission to fill the earth with children who would love God and each other. Getting back to the basics is sometimes started by going back to the basics.

The night before Jesus chose who His 12 disciples would be, He drew away in the wilderness. He and three of His disciples were alone on a mountain when He had His transfiguration encounter with Moses and Elijah. In the agonizing moments prior to His arrest and crucifixion, we see Him in a garden on His face before His Abba Father. Often, Jesus drew away. If He *needed* to do this, how much more do we *need* it? If we see Him doing this before major decisions and events, how much more do we need it before we bite the big bullets, make the big jumps, and sign the dotted lines?

You may not be able to take a week and head for the beach, but you *can* take an hour and go to the park. You may not be able to fly to Maui, but you can walk the neighborhood early, before too much else is happening. Deciding to get up 30 minutes earlier and spend time listening to worship music and reading your Bible will profit you more than you can imagine. Your garden may have to be your back deck, your back porch, or your back balcony. Your Eden may have to be found in the local library underneath a set of headphones that drown out all the distractions. Some busy mothers have become so creative and desperate that a trip to the supermarket without the little ones turns the produce section into paradise. All of us yearn for a little place in this busy world to have all to ourselves. Such a place is a valuable piece of real estate. If you find it, cherish it, and use it—you are blessed indeed. Wives please don't hate me for this, but this may be another reason that your husbands are mesmerized by chasing a little white ball with a thin steel stick. A golf course is usually a beautiful place where the smell of green life fills the air. A lot of guys just need to work on their *follow-through,* and I'm not talking about their golf swing. They need to *follow through* on the yearning in their soul that seems to be placated a little bit on the golf course. They are lonely for God. Like anything else in life, golf is more enjoyable when you purpose to walk alone with God. All the course designs are plagiarisms anyway. The green idea was God's to start with. We know that guys are adventuresome. It's the dominion that God placed inside of them that has programmed them to conquer, to see what's over the next hill, to know what the surface of the moon looks like. Go for it, guys! Don't stop until you come face-to-face with God! Adam heard God's voice in the garden, and you can as well. He's calling for you to meet with Him, fellowship with Him, talk with Him, and listen to Him.

I believe this is the call of God on everyone's life. It is important that everyone discover what God's plan for their life is, including you. You may be called to work in the marketplace, the classroom, city hall, a construction crew, laboratory, YMCA, NASA, the White House, or thousands of other spheres of influence. If it's in line with your destiny, you will experience a fulfillment of being in the right place at the right time. I am not saying that this feeling will stick with you every moment of every day. You *will* have challenges. But the feeling will be strong enough and long enough for you to know that you know that you have discovered destiny. Make the most out of what you have and where you are. As you invite Him into more of your life, you will feel more at home with Him. It was not Eden that made Adam's life complete, it was God. You can know the God of Adam as intimately as he did. Augustus Hare, an English clergyman, wrote in 1827: "To Adam, Paradise was home. To the good among his descendants, home is paradise." Start experiencing Eden today in your own home. Make up your mind to reclaim what your great, great, great...granddad Adam lost. Father is just a breath away. Breathe a prayer and bid Him come.

TWENTY

MADE TO PRAISE

The climax of God's happiness is the delight
He takes in the echoes of His excellence
in the praises of His people.

John Piper

Have you ever watched the spontaneous bursts of enthusiasm on a Saturday afternoon when a touchdown is scored by the home team? People simply cannot contain themselves. They wear their team colors and wildly wave posters, banners, and pom-poms in the air. Shouts and screams can be heard beyond the stadium. No one thinks it is a strange thing either. It is expected that we fanatically support our team. After all, that is what a fan is—a fanatic! The Book of Psalms repeatedly calls us to be fanatics for the Lord. The last verse of Psalms sums it up: *Let everything that has breath praise the LORD. Praise the LORD!*

Sir William Temple, who served as the Archbishop of Canterbury in the early part of the 20th century, made a beautiful assessment of the big picture when he said, "To worship is to quicken the conscience by the holiness of God, to purge the imagination by the beauty of God, to open the heart to the love of God, and to devote the will to the purpose of God." Heavenly Father gave you the breath of life, and you are to use it for Him. You are called to live a life of praise to God. This means there is to be nothing about your life that should not reflect gratitude and awe toward God. Use your breath to praise God! Every time that your lungs fill with air and you expel air out of your body, it should flow from a heart that loves God. Praise is a powerful thing. When you are facing obstacles in your path, begin to praise God and watch them shrink before your eyes. He is always greater than that which you face. You need to become so thoroughly convinced of the greatness of God that every cell of your being is calling His name. Soak your DNA with the truth that you were made by Him and for Him. The world operates by the adage that "seeing is believing." However, you, child of God, are to operate by the axiom that "believing is seeing."

Whatever you praise becomes your passion. Let your whole being become possessed by God. Let your heart beat for Him. Let your mind dwell on Him. Let your ears listen for His voice. Let your eyes look for Him in everything you face. This is your destiny. This is what you were made for. You are here because of Him. You live, move, and have your being in Him. Love Him and live for Him. This is where the meaning of life is found. The foundation of your existence, when all the fluff is swept aside, is knowing Almighty God through His Son Jesus Christ. Every time you praise God, you are affirming the reason of your existence. Every act of worship is a demonstration of your destiny. Praise Him, reader! Praise Him!

As you magnify God, you minimize your problems. Through your praise, you see Him as bigger than the mountain before you, greater than the storm raging around you. Just begin praising God when trouble comes! Praise Him for being wisdom in the face of tough decisions. Praise Him for being your healer when you are facing sickness. Praise Him for being your provider when finances are thin and you have more month than you have money. Praise Him for being with you when others are walking away from you. Praise Him for protecting you when danger is lurking near. Praise Him for being your Shepherd when you are choosing which path to take. Praise Him for being love when anger has left its mark on you. Praise Him for being peace when confusion rolls in like a fog around you. Praise Him for being joy when depression stalks your emotions. Praise Him for being grace to you when weakness has a hold on you. Praise Him! Praise Him! Praise Him! He will become to you what you praise Him to be. You have breath—use it to praise the Lord. You were made to praise.

When it is all said and done and the eternity we await welcomes us, we will still be praising Him. A million light years from now, when this world as we know it has been changed forever, we will still be praising Him. Man was made to live in a paradise with God. Adam awakened in paradise and had to leave it. Jesus left paradise to come to Earth to die for us. Before He breathed His last breath, He assured the repentant thief with the words: *And Jesus said to him, "Assuredly, I say to you, today you will be with Me in Paradise"* (Lk 23:43). The Apostle Paul had an experience where he was allowed to see the glories of the world that await the believer. He described the experience in the following verse: *...how he was caught up into Paradise and heard inexpressible words, which it is not lawful for a man to utter* (2 Co 12:4). Jesus gives this promise to believers who live the overcoming life: *"He who has an ear, let him hear what the Spirit says to the churches. To him who overcomes I will give to eat from the tree of life, which is in the midst of the Paradise of God"* (Re 2:7).

When Adam experienced the first breath, he awakened in Eden, the place of pleasure. He lived by a river. He lived in the presence of God. He saw God's face and heard God's voice. He ate from the tree of life. He served God. This was his destiny, and it is ours. Read the following passage that describes our ultimate destination.

And he showed me a pure river of water of life, clear as crystal, proceeding from the throne of God and of the Lamb. In the middle of its street, and on either side of the river, was the tree of life, which bore twelve fruits, each tree yielding its fruit every month. The leaves of the tree were for the healing of the nations. And there shall be no more curse, but the throne of God and of the Lamb shall be in it, and His servants shall serve Him. They shall see His face, and His name shall be on their foreheads. There shall be no night there: They need no lamp nor light of the sun, for the Lord God gives them light. And they shall reign forever and ever.

Revelation 22:1-5

As it was in the beginning, so shall it be in the end. God's original intention will be realized. In Eden, there was one tree of life. In heaven, our future destination, there will be two trees of life. A double blessing awaits us. There will be the healing of the nations. All God's children will see His face, hear His voice, and live in His presence by His river. There Jesus, the last Adam, will enjoy a great wedding banquet with His wife, the church. What a glorious time it will be in Father's house! This is the eternal home that we are headed toward. It is not Eden—it is better than Eden!

In addition, Father God's desire will be realized when He has children from all around the earth gathered before Him praising Him and enjoying Him. What a beautiful scene is described for us in the following passage.

After these things I looked, and behold, a great multitude which no one could number, of all nations, tribes, peoples, and tongues, standing before the throne and before the Lamb, clothed with white robes, with palm branches in their hands, and crying out with a loud voice, saying, "Salvation belongs to our God who sits on the throne, and to the Lamb!" All the angels stood around the throne and the elders and the four living creatures, and fell on their faces before the throne and worshiped God, saying:

"Amen! Blessing and glory and wisdom,
Thanksgiving and honor and power and might,
Be to our God forever and ever. Amen."

Revelation 7:9-12

This passage concerns those who not only lived for Father but were willing to die for Him. As I mentioned early in this book, what we are willing to die for defines us. I encourage you to examine your heart and see if its compass is pointing toward Father God. Everything originated with Him, and everything will be summed up in Him! What an awesome destiny awaits the child of God! It is my prayer that you have given your life to Jesus Christ and know God as your Heavenly Father. If you have not, why not pray right now and ask Jesus to come into your life and save you? Confess Him as the Lord of your life. He died for you—live for Him! He gave you your first breath, and He will determine when you breathe your last breath. Breathe them all for Him!

The fulfillment for which your craving heart yearns is found when God breathes His life upon your life. Living for the God who gives you life is why you are here! To settle for something less is to live away from your life's grandest goal. If you are hungry to experience the breath of God upon your life, position yourself as Adam was before God breathed on him. See yourself as dust, dead and lifeless, and ask God to fill you with His life. His existence is the reason for your existence. Without His life, there is no life!

God, who made the world and everything in it, since He is Lord of heaven and earth, does not dwell in temples made with hands. Nor is He worshiped with men's hands, as though He needed anything, since He

gives to all life, breath, and all things (Ac 17:24-25). He has given you
the breath of life to live on this earth. There is a stewardship of the
breath of life. It should be valued and used for the glory of God
from whence it came. The breath of God experience is about coming alive to God. It worked for Adam; it will work for you. May He
breathe on you and may your lungs burn with a white-hot, passionate love for Him! May you praise God with your every breath, and
when your last breath is breathed, may it praise His name!

APPENDIX

Moving Beyond Eden

And people who do not know the Lord ask why in the world we waste our lives as missionaries. They forget that they too are expending their lives...and when the bubble has burst, they will have nothing of eternal significance to show for the years they have wasted.

Nate Saint, age 32
Martyred in Ecuador on the mission field in 1955

MOVING BEYOND EDEN

Author's Note: I desired to add this teaching on the four rivers that flowed out of Eden. It is certainly symbolic in its scope, but I think it will encourage you to realize that God had planned life beyond Eden for Adam as well. He was to impact the whole globe by following the Spirit of God inside of him. This is our call as well. Enjoy this little extra ride on the river that flowed out of Eden.

Several years ago on a family vacation to Fort Walton Beach, Florida, my youngest sons, Elliott and Nathan, and I drove across the bay to Destin. I was keeping a promise to them by spending a day at Big Kahuna's water park. We enjoyed floating along a long, winding river. We slid down the slides. I went flying down one of the super slides and felt the friction on my body as speed mounted and I exploded into the pool below. From there, we went to all the other exciting adventures that filled the park. A few hours after my super slide experience, I happened to rub my hand along my swimsuit on my backside. This is when I made a startling, embarrassing, turn-the-face-red discovery. I had experienced a severe blowout! The seat of my swimsuit had virtually disappeared, but my posterior anatomy had not. Having discovered this *split*, I wanted to *split*. I quickly moved to a place where my back was to the wall. It then occurred to me that I had been bending, jumping, running, and swimming all over the park, unknowingly exposing myself. This really gave new meaning to the name "Big Kahuna's." I could only imagine the various conversations that had been taking place among people in the park concerning the man ignorantly streaking around the park in his ripped-open swimsuit. Maybe they thought it was a new fashion trend. I can see it now, *"Full Moon*

153

Swimwear, for those who don't want to be *behind* the times." Why didn't somebody tell me? In a sense, we all have made fools of ourselves as we have played in the water park of life. We drift along life's river, often unknowingly exposing ourselves in the pursuit of pleasure. Adam and Eve lived by a river, and it was fun until they sinned and realized they were naked and ashamed. Then they tried fig leaves but found that they were useless. Life on the river can teach us a lot if we will wise up and listen. We need to learn to *wisely* enjoy the river.

Throughout history, people have chosen to live by rivers. The river is a place of life and movement. It provides fish to eat, water to drink, and navigation to the regions beyond. A river will eventually empty into something bigger than it is—the ocean. The first man and woman, Adam and Eve, lived by a river. They were river folk!

In the New Testament, we see the outflow or release of the Spirit and life of God from the lives of believers. This is the power to serve God and others. The Holy Spirit is not to be contained within us just for our own sake. He is to be released through us for the sake of others. As I heard Dr. Boyce Albright, a deacon in a church where I once served, say, "We are not to be reservoirs like the Dead Sea; we are to be rivers like the Jordan." Do you know a rut is just a place where a river once flowed? We are to get out of our spiritual ruts and jump back into the river. Jesus taught us that the Holy Spirit was to be like a river flowing out of our lives. *He who believes in Me, as the Scripture has said, out of his heart will flow rivers of living water. But this He spoke concerning the Spirit, whom those believing in Him would receive; for the Holy Spirit was not yet given, because Jesus was not yet glorified* (Jo 7:38-39).

As a believer in Jesus Christ, the presence of God lives inside of you. You have rivers of living water flowing out of you to bring the blessing of God to others around you. Eternal life is inside of you through the Spirit of God. This is the same Spirit that filled the first Adam and the same Spirit that resurrected the last Adam. Jesus described the Holy Spirit's movement in and through our lives like that of a flowing river. Adam was full of the Spirit of God as he lived in the Garden of Eden; he also lived by a river. In fact, the river in Eden tells us a lot about living life in the Spirit.

Throughout the Scripture, a river is often used as an illustration of the place where God's presence is flowing. The river that flowed through Eden certainly was flowing in the place of God's presence. In the Book of Ezekiel, the prophet writes of a river that flowed out of the temple. Again, this was a place of God's presence. In the Book of Revelation, the Apostle John concludes with the description of the river that flows out of the throne of God. The three rivers seen in Eden, in Ezekiel's temple, and in eternity are all associated with the presence of God. There was a river that went out of Eden, which broke up into four riverheads. Each of the Hebrew names of these rivers carries some meaning about our destiny in God.

Now a river went out of Eden to water the garden, and from there it parted and became four riverheads. The name of the first is Pishon; it is the one which skirts the whole land of Havilah, where there is gold. And the gold of that land is good. Bdellium and the onyx stone are there. The name of the second river is Gihon; it is the one which goes around the whole land of Cush. The name of the third river is Hiddekel; it is the one which goes toward the east of Assyria. The fourth river is the Euphrates.

Genesis 2:10-14

Let me share some symbolic meanings about the four rivers that flowed out of the river in Eden.

Multiplication

The first river, *Pishon*, means "to spring up." Therefore, I call it the river of multiplication. When you get in the river of God's presence and start being carried and moved by it, one of the places it is going to carry you is called Increase. It is the place of productivity. It is where multiplication takes place. Adam and Eve were commanded to multiply and fill the earth—that's increase.

We are told that the Pishon flowed through the land of Havilah where there was gold—*good gold*. Bdellium and onyx stones were there. In other words, where it flows you will see treasures. Gold is one of the most precious, valuable natural commodities on Earth. The Bible teaches us that when we walk with God and flow in the river, we are a blessed people. The river of God will carry us to the places where the most valuable things can be found. Gold and precious stones have to be mined, so they are hidden treasures. They are there, but they have to be found. When you discover treasure on the banks of the river, it is very exciting. I do not think that we children of God should be embarrassed to tell people that we are blessed. We are sons and daughters of our Heavenly Father; the cattle on a thousand hills belong to Him. The Book of Psalms teaches us that God takes pleasure in the prosperity of His servants.

> *Let them shout for joy and be glad,*
> *Who favor my righteous cause;*
> *And let them say continually,*
> *"Let the LORD be magnified,*
> *Who has pleasure in the prosperity of His servant"* (Ps 35:27).

The first place He put Adam was in the place of pleasure, Eden. One of the places the river of God flows into is increase, prosperity, and multiplication. Don't let your greed take over here. This does not mean that when you serve God you are guaranteed a life of luxury surrounded by silver, gold, and precious stones. You may have those things; just don't let them have you. The Father loves to bless His children even at the risk that those blessings will be used against Him. Read the following warning that the Lord gives Israel prior to receiving the inheritance in the promised land.

> *Beware that you do not forget the LORD your God by not keeping His commandments, His judgments, and His statutes which I command you today, lest—when you have eaten and are full, and have built beautiful houses and dwell in them; and when your herds and your flocks multiply, and your silver and your gold are multiplied, and all that you have is multiplied; when your heart is lifted up, and you forget the LORD your God who brought you out of the land of Egypt, from the house of bondage; who led you through that great and terrible wilderness, in which were fiery serpents and scorpions and thirsty land where there was no water; who brought water for you out of the flinty rock; who fed you in the wilderness with manna, which your fathers did not know, that He might humble you and that He might test you, to do you good in the end—then you say in your heart, "My power and the might of my hand have gained me this wealth."*
>
> Deuteronomy 8:11-17

Guard your heart against greed and the tendency to take credit for your success. The truth is, neither you nor I could take our next breath without Him. We could not tie our shoes without Him.

James, the brother of our Lord, reminds us every good gift comes from Him. Actually, He is the greatest treasure. Knowing Him is better than owning the whole stock market.

The river flowing out of the place of intimacy with the Lord will carry you to the places where those things God values are hidden. Riding on this river will help you discover the true treasure. Start looking beneath the surface, and you will see what I mean. When you look into the eyes of your spouse and children, think of the treasures that they are to Father God. You will see a glistening greater than that of diamonds when you fellowship among God's people. Learn to look beyond the surface for the hidden treasure in their hearts. You will see the value of God in the life of the outcast and stranger for whom Christ died. These are occasions when we see the increase and productivity that God promises. These are occasions when the really good gold is to be found. Natural gold has been placed here just to help us in our search for the true treasures.

Biblical prosperity means that I will always have whatever I need to do the will of God. Ride the river Pishon, and you will discover this to be true.

Maturity

The second river that flowed out of Eden, *Gihon*, means "to burst forth." It is the picture of a river whose water rises until it overflows the barriers that have contained it. I call this the river of maturity. It is the place of bursting forth when you finally advance through the struggle. This river takes you to that point when you are finally propelled into what God has ordained for you. This happens when you pass the test and advance to the next level on this river. How exhilarating it is to pass the test and move down the river!

This river is a picture of breakthrough. It is a picture of bursting out of and going beyond the boundaries. It is a picture of advancing through a struggle. The river is contained until it gets to a point where it cannot be contained; then, it bursts forth.

When you get in the river with God, maturity is part of the process. Maturity is learning to advance through a struggle without violating love. We always think we are ready to advance before we are, and think we shouldn't have to wait as long as we have to wait. With excitement and zeal, we want to spring *out* before it is spring-*time*. Springtime follows the time of containment, development, and dealing with struggles. God first enlarges *us* and then releases us into the enlarged *place*. When He gives the green light, we burst forth.

Solomon wrote in Proverbs 3:10 that when we trust in the Lord and refuse to become wise in our own eyes, our vats would burst forth with new wine. *So your barns will be filled with plenty, And your vats will overflow with new wine.* In Isaiah 58:8, the prophet reminds us when we begin ministering to those in need, our own healing will burst forth speedily. *Then your light shall break forth like the morning, Your healing shall spring forth speedily, And your righteousness shall go before you; The glory of the LORD shall be your rear guard.* The bursting forth after being contained is a picture of momentum—being propelled ahead and shifted to a new place in the river.

By all means, wait on God to open the gates for your advancement. Sometimes we are deceived and think it is the enemy holding us back when it is God doing so. The enemy always wants to hasten us. He is a pusher. The Holy Spirit leads; the devil shoves. Once we identify our destiny and know we are called of God, we must be wary of the enemy tempting us to run ahead of God.

I believe that it works like this: if you run ahead of God before you are ready, then in five years, you will not be much farther along in your destiny than you are right now. But, if you will learn to wait on God and walk with God through the process, let Him nurture, mature, and develop your character, then five years from now you will be light years ahead of where you would have been by any other means. Because you have been contained and have learned to honor boundaries, you will experience the breaking forth that occurs in the river of maturity. You will go much farther, much higher, and accomplish much more for the kingdom because you were willing to submit to the boundaries that God prescribed for you.

Miracles

The third river, *Hiddekel*, (commonly known by its Greek name, Tigris) means "to press in or to thrust in." This is the river where things move quickly. This is not just advance but rapid advance. I call this the river of miracles. This is the place of exhilaration and acceleration where things that are not humanly possible begin to happen. When you wait upon the Lord and the time comes, He will furnish the power needed for you to break through into your destiny. He will open the doors before you. He will make a way when there seems to be no way. I live very near Wilson Dam, which is one of the dams on the Tennessee River system, managed by the Tennessee Valley Authority. When TVA opens up the gates on the dam, you had better not be in the way! It is an awesome sight to see the power of the water rushing from the place where it has been contained to the place where it can race downstream. During the process of the water exploding through those gates, huge turbines are turned which generate electricity. The electrical energy produced lights up much of Northwest Alabama.

It is not uncommon for a person who has been "in holding" by the hand of God to experience powerful miracles in their life once God opens the door. This acceleration literally propels us into the next level with God.

A couple of years ago, our family was invited to a Fourth of July outing on Wilson Lake. There were several families from our congregation there to enjoy the day together. Good food, fun, and fellowship filled the air. Eventually, I found myself on an inner tube being pulled by a powerful WaveRunner™. It was a lot of fun, especially when the driver would make a circle, allowing me to ride out across the wake and glide across the surface of the water like an ice skater on ice. Then it happened! I made the fatal error of boasting to my friend Dan, who was driving the WaveRunner™, that I was surprised he could not throw me off. I had seen him throw others off earlier in the day and assumed that he had been unable to do the same to me. Oh, boy, did I regret allowing those stupid words to escape my lips. I saw the look in his eyes when I spoke those daring words. The gauntlet had been thrown down; the challenge had been made. It was man-to-man combat. He took off with me in tow. I gripped the inner tube as if glued to it. We went racing down the river, headed toward the pier where all our friends stood watching their preacher exhibit his aquatic skills on the mighty Tennessee River. As we approached, Dan held the throttle wide open. We were moving at high speed. Suddenly, he thrust the steering bar hard to the left and the inner tube to which I was attached was shot out across the wave to the right like a ball shot from a cannon. It was the first time in my life that I experienced what the astronauts surely feel when they are hurled into outer space. With my knuckles turning white and my eyes closed tight, I held on for dear life. I knew that the laws of physics would intervene when the slack I had gained in the rope suddenly came to an end. When the rope finally came to the point where it snapped me back the opposite direction, I was thrown without mercy across the surface of the water like a skipping rock. The inner tube went one way and I went the other. It felt as if my body were rolling at the speed of light. I heard my bones popping as my body twisted and my mind writhed in wonder at what was happening to me. No one was able to count the number of times I tumbled, but I covered what seemed like several hundred feet of water that felt like concrete. My childhood flashed before me. Witnesses testified that they had never seen someone hang on so long and then thrown so far. As I lay on the surface of the water floating like a dead fish, I remembered what Solomon had written about pride going before destruction and a haughty spirit before a fall. Did he ever get that one right! My congregants stared in shock wondering if their preacher was dead or alive. I have never *walked* on water, but I can truthfully say I have *rolled* on water! I get sore again just telling the story. This story represents the acceleration we experience through times of miraculous breakthrough. During these times, we are thrust by the hand of a higher power into a new realm of the river. Remember to buckle up and hang on when your time of breakthrough comes!

Patiently waiting within the boundaries will release you into the place of blessing. However, do not honor the place of boundaries just because you want to get the miracles. Realize that the miracles are given to carry you into the fulfillment of God's purposes for your life. Don't get into pride either. It will get you into trouble and a ride of a different sort. Humbly wait on God, and He will exalt you in due time.

Ministry

The fourth river that flowed out of Eden was the Euphrates. The origin of the Hebrew word *Euphrates* is unknown. It may be translated "to break forth" or "flowering." I call it the river of ministry because it is the river that disperses. It is like a flower when it opens up and begins to share its fragrance with those who are around it. When it opens up, it also produces fruit.

This is the river where we are *filled* so that we can be *spilled*. I thank God for the rapid river, for it carries us to the place where we can see fruit produced. We need the river of ministry because it is not just about being people who hang out in the river with no regard to anyone else. We do not need to be selfish about the river. We do not need to be river junkies. The river is moving to something bigger, and it is wrong to make the river itself the destination. The river is not the destination. It is the means to your destination, the place of increase, the place of maturity, the place of the miraculous, and the place of ministry. In order to be all God created us to be, we need to spend time traveling on each of these four rivers that flow out of the river in Eden. The combined energies and lessons of the four rivers create balance in each of us.

My wife and I sleep with a sound machine playing beside our bed each night. It produces several different sounds, but the one we choose to sleep by is the sound of a trickling river. It is so peaceful and natural. As Adam took his first breath, he could hear the trickle of the river. He could hear the river running. He was a river man, and deep inside so are you. Something inside each of us yearns to be by the river of God. Be sure you are wearing the covering God has provided. Fig leafs will only cause you to have a blowout!

I love to live on the brink of eternity.

David Brainerd

NOTES

1. "Pluto May Have Three Moons, Not One," ABC: Space and Astronomy News, http://www.abc.net.au/science/news/space/SpaceRepublish_1495007.htm (accessed January 23, 2006).

2. Imperfect Estimate Claims Universe Has 70 Sextillion Stars, By Robert Roy Britt, Senior Science Writer, posted July 22, 2003. http://www.space.com/scienceastronomy/star_count_030722.html (accessed February 22, 2006).

3. Rutherford and the Nucleus found at http://www.schoolscience.co.uk/content/5/physics/particles/partich1pg1x.html (accessed February 22, 2006).

4. Matthew Yi, "Livermore Supercomputer Ranked as World's Fastest," *San Francisco Chronicle,* June 22, 2005, http://www.sfgate.com/cgi-bin/article.cgi?file=/chronicle/archive/2005/06/22/BUG93DC77916.DTL&type=business (accessed February 22, 2006).

5. Paul Kallender, "Japan Aims for World's Fastest Supercomputer," IDG News Service, 05/31/05.

6. Peter S. Williams, "A Change of Mind for Antony Flew" http://www.arn.org/docs/williams/pw_antonyflew.htm (accessed February 22, 2006).

7. "Scientists v. God," JokeCenter.com, http://www.jokecenter.com/jokes/Religion/5105.htm (accessed February 22, 2006).

8. Martin Luther King, *Strength to Love* (New York: Harper & Row, 1963).

9. Robertson's *Word Pictures in the New Testament,* Electronic Database. Copyright © 1997, 2003 by Biblesoft, Inc. Robertson's *Word Pictures in the New Testament.* Copyright © 1985 by Broadman Press.

10. *Theological Wordbook of the Old Testament.* Copyright © 1980 by The Moody Bible Institute of Chicago. All rights reserved. Used by permission.

11. "Revival Sermons," SermonIndex.net, http://www.sermonindex.net/modules/mydownloads/viewcat.php?cid=64 (accessed February 22, 2006).

12. *The Biblical Illustrator.* Copyright © 2002 AGES and Biblesoft, Inc.

13. Harold Myra and Marshall Shelly, *The Leadership Secrets of Billy Graham* (Grand Rapids: Zondervan, 2005) p. 23.

14. Ibid., p. 22

15. Sermonillustrations.com

To contact Eddie Lawrence about conferences and speaking engagements email—eddie@firstbreathministries.com, or phone (256) 767-4124 to speak with his secretary. For information about other resources by the author, visit www.firstbreathministries.com. Other information about Dr. Lawrence's pastorate can be found at www.LifeatFaith.com.

To sign up for email updates on Eddie's writing, speaking engagements, and resources, visit: www.firstbreathministries.com and click on the sign-up feature.

Prayer requests or other enquiries also may be sent to info@firstbreathministries.com.

Eddie's Breath of God blog is:
http://eddielawrence.blogspot.com

Mail can be sent to:

First Breath Ministries
P.O. Box 1228
Killen, Alabama 35645